LIFE BEYOND CONVENTIONS
Journey of a Small Town Girl to a Big City

LIFE BEYOND CONVENTIONS

Journey of a Small Town Girl to a Big City

Dimple Saxena

KALPAZ

ISBN: 978-93-5128-020-0

Price: ₹ 180

First Published 2013

Published by

Kalpaz Publications
C-30, Satyawati Nagar,
Delhi - 110052
E-mail: kalpaz@hotmail.com Ph.: 9212142040

Laser Typesetting : Rajender Vashist, Delhi
Printed at: G. Print Process, Delhi

Cataloging in Publication Data--DK
Courtesy: D.K. Agencies (P) Ltd. <docinfo@dkagencies.com>

Saxena, Dimple.
Life beyond conventions : journey of a small town girl to a big city / Dimple Saxena.
p. cm.
Novel.
ISBN 9789351280200

1. Yamunanagar (India : District).--Fiction. 2. Girls--Fiction. 3. Migration, Internal--India--Haryana--Fiction. 4. Indic fiction (English). I. Title.

DDC 823.92 23

"Oh! Lord (Ganesha), of huge body and curved elephant trunk, whose brilliance is equal to billions of suns, always remove all obstacles from my endeavours."

Dedication

I dedicate this book to my family.

I want to thank my husband for supporting me in writing this book. Thanks to my friends and family for their suggestions at all stages. Thanks to my editors Tilottama Bhalla and Monisha Chattopadhyay for their valuable work and suggestions. I love my city Yamuna Nagar and its people who inspired me to pen down my thoughts.

Contents

Introduction

Before you read further, let me take you through Yamuna Nagar

Yamuna Nagar is a small town in Haryana, situated as the name suggests, on the banks of the River Yamuna. The lifestyle of the people of Yamuna Nagar is simple despite the fact that many families run their own businesses. Rarely would you find the quality of diplomacy in the people of Yamuna Nagar. They share their ancestral lineage with the people of Punjab and Haryana and like the people of their ethnic origin, they are bold, loud and outspoken. In this small town, people live their lives and die with their dreams unfulfilled. But then, there are those who live to see another day and fulfil their dreams in spite all the struggles they have encountered.

Every year, thousands of people from small towns flock to big cities to fulfil their dreams and make it big in life. Their dreams and achievements may not matter to people in the metro cities, as for them, they are another herd of migrants who have walked into their space. On the contrary, if we look at it from the perspective of a small town dreamer, it is really an achievement.

The protagonist of this story, Naina, hails from the small town of Yamuna Nagar and belongs to a conventional and conservative family, where struggles and restrictions are a part and parcel of her early life. It is her determination and perseverance that paves the way for her to realise her big dreams in the so called big city of Gurgaon.

Her experiences in life made her a firm believer of the fact that "Life is a roller coaster ride". It is full of ups and downs but if one has the courage and will power to win, there is no looking back.

Naina's story is similar to the stories of many girls or boys who belong to small towns and migrate to big cities for life changing opportunities. Their lives change every moment.

Prologue

I went to the bedroom and kissed Jaison on the cheek. Jaison, who was in deep slumber, woke up, pulled me into bed beside him and said, "Sweetheart, you've come back after three months. I won't let you go anywhere now. Every year you go to the US on your official trip and put me in exile. Last night when I saw you at the airport, I was so excited I just could not stop myself from hugging you tightly."

"Well, now I'm here and with you, so you can hug me as many times as you want. Why are you saying that I put you in exile each time I go to the US? What about the time you went to Australia and left me all alone here in Gurgaon?" I teased him.

We hugged and kissed each other. Jaison went back to sleep but I couldn't sleep because I was suffering from jet lag. While he slept, I came out of the room and sat on the steps with a cup of piping hot coffee. It was a cold day in December. Heavy mist clouded the air. Though barely visible, I could make out some trees standing tall and unruffled, an electric pole loaded with wires, cars parked in the lane opposite and big houses, all covered with mist. Many things went through my mind within that split second.

My mind worked overtime and I tried to relate to the two Nainas from two different worlds - one who had recently returned from USA and the other, a small town girl from Yamuna Nagar who was striving hard to fulfil her dreams.

The journey of the past six years had completely transformed my life. Six years ago I had come to this city with empty hands but with a lot of confidence and zeal to achieve something in my life. I have not forgotten the hardships that I have had to encounter to reach where I am today. When I think of my childhood, thousands of memories flash through my mind like scenes from a film that I have seen many times.

1

The Past: My Family

My story begins in a typical household in Yamuna Nagar. Our house was big enough to accommodate thirteen family members. It had four bedrooms, one hall, a kitchen, a store room and two big verandas. I remember my family sitting in the veranda together and sharing their sorrows and joys. I cannot forget my father sitting there looking crestfallen when he found life hopeless and bleak.

Let me introduce you to the different members in my family. We had all sorts of people under one roof.

Mother worked nonstop from five in the morning to eleven at night because we didn't have domestic help. She had the responsibility of running the household as well as of looking after her two children along with her three brothers-in-law and two sisters-in-law. No one ever realised her selfless hard work in looking after all of us and the sacrifices she made every day. She had been taught by her parents that women are born to make sacrifices and that they are blessed with enormous energy to run an entire household. Every morning she had to cook thirty to forty chapattis and a big pan full of daal. She cooked the same quantity of food two times a day, in addition to cleaning her four bedroom house and washing clothes for the entire household.

Father was the eldest of the lot. He was the one who ran the whole show in our family. His demeanour was tough and he looked strict and disciplined which frightened everyone. We, his children, and his younger brothers and sisters were so terrified of him that we did not even dare to step out of house until he had left for his office. He took care of the obvious responsibilities of his brothers, sisters, children and wife. Every day, he had to put in four to five hours overtime to meet all the household expenses. He worked from nine in the morning to ten thirty at night. When he returned home at night, pin drop silence descended over the entire household. We all made sure that we had stepped inside, grabbed our books and kept our heads firmly buried in them to make him feel that we were studying.

I'd like to tell my readers that I cannot repay even an iota of what my parents have done for me. Parents are the only people in this world who stand by us through thick and thin.

My second uncle Nagendra was a shopkeeper who sold stationery and photo frames. He was the funniest person in our family. He didn't care about anything in his life. If anyone ever asked him what he had thought about his future, he would reply, "God has already planned everything and He will take care of us. Then why should we worry?" Nagendra Uncle was the nicest among all the other uncles. He used to open his shop at approximately nine in the morning and closed it by about twelve every night. His shop timings gave people the impression that he was the busiest person on this earth. It's of course yet another story that most of his customers praised him for not delivering products on time! The name of his shop was 'Nagen Hotch Potch'.

The other two uncles and aunts were studying in college. My fourth uncle Jeetendra was in the matric class. I used to feel awkward as there wasn't much age difference between Jeet Uncle and me. I couldn't understand how one could have such young uncles. What I didn't know at that age was that in earlier times, families were larger as people used to have many children. There could also be situations when mothers-in-law and daughters-in-law delivered babies at the same time.

My grandmother Rajeshwari was a housewife. She loved my brother Priyanshu very much as he was the first boy of the next generation in her family. Priyanshu was sweet and cute and very intelligent. I think he has been blessed with a brilliant brain. He takes only a few minutes to solve a brain teaser while I may take an eternity to solve it. He is not a bookworm like me but does everything in a relaxed manner without putting in too much of an effort. Being mischievous, he was at the receiving end more often than me. I remember that in our childhood, my mother would tell my father about his latest act of mischief and then, my father would thrash him. Gradually, however, Priyanshu became indifferent about the beatings.

We had a very strict upbringing and as a result, always got an equal share of love and beating from our parents. They felt they had to do this because they wanted us to excel in our lives.

> This story revolves around me. I, being a small town girl, had a pocket full of dreams that were beyond the imagination of my family members. I wanted to see the world that existed beyond the orthodox walls of home. As I grew up, my dreams started growing within me. I envied the fact that girls in metro cities lived lives that were more fulfilling than ours. I always wished to wear short skirts instead of the traditional salwar kameez, to fly in an aeroplane instead of travelling in the general compartment of a train, to drive my own car, to live an independent life and much more. Yet here I was, part of a conservative family, where there was lack of transparency and freedom of expression – consequently, many things were left unsaid.

It took me a lot of courage to overcome hurdles and break barriers. It was difficult for me to spread my wings and fly high, but I did it. Restrictions gave birth to ambitions. Using all my skills and resources to bring out the best in me, I embarked on my journey from a small town towards a big city to fulfil my dreams.

2

My Childhood

Our bedroom was of an average size. In one part of the room there was a double bed which had been custom made to fit the room. My parents, Priyanshu and I slept on it for almost ten years. At arm's length from the bed, there was a cupboard. On the other side of the bed there was a full length mirror placed over a tiny wooden table. Some pairs of footwear were kept under our bed. A large poster of the Indian goddess Ma Durga adorned a portion of the wall above the tube-light.

Priyanshu and I were in deep slumber when my Dad shouted and woke me from my sweet dreams. "Get up kids, it's already five o'clock." I opened my eyes which were still full of sleep and looked around. I could see nothing but a bright white tube-light in my room.

"Get up and go and wash your eyes. Bring me your maths book and we'll solve some addition sums."

I went to the bathroom, washed my eyes with cold water and then took out the maths book from my school bag. Meanwhile, my parents were still busy waking up my sleepy brother.

"Get up Priyanshu, get up."

He got up and went to the washroom, hardly able to make his tiny legs move. His eyes were drowsy as though he was drunk. My father started teaching me. Twenty minutes passed but Priyanshu had not joined us. My father knocked on the door and shouted, "Priyanshu, I know you are sleeping inside. Come out, today we'll finish your English dictation. You've scored very low marks in your class test."

The little maharaja came out of the washroom and sat with us with his little English book.

I continued with my sums and Priyanshu started learning the English words in his lesson, as after thirty minutes, he would take dictation from my father.

"Ok, both of you carry on and I'll go to the washroom. Then we'll continue after I come back." My father was back after ten minutes and Priyanshu woke up in shock as his right cheek was stinging and it had turned red.

"How dare you go to sleep again? I told you to learn the English words." Priyanshu started crying, rubbing his eyes with his tiny hands all the while.

After two hours, we started getting ready for school. While Priyanshu and I were getting ready, my father made us stuff large mouthfuls of bread which we were made to swallow with big glasses of milk. I felt irritated.

Priyanshu was still busy making excuses. "I won't go to school Mom, you should first buy me a good pencil box and look at this pair of socks - they are of different sizes." My father slapped him again.

After all this commotion in the morning, we finally managed to get ready for school. One thing I hated every morning was that I would have to wait for my turn for the washroom. We were thirteen people in our joint family. Everyone would want to run in at the same time. One would go in as soon as the other came out. I often felt like throwing up when it was my turn, as the others had used it continuously before me. The only time we could use the washroom easily was during the afternoon when there was no one there.

My father gave us a ride on his bicycle till we reached the main road. "Repeat these English words five times after me. We'll practice until the bus comes," he ordered.

A few minutes later the bus came and the conductor lifted us, one by one, into the bus.

My father rode back home. Once he reached, he rang the doorbell continuously and impatiently, shouting all the while, "Open, open".

My mother left the kitchen and ran to the main door shouting, "I'm coming, can't you wait for a second? Can't you see I'm busy making breakfast for everyone in the family?"

My father rushed past her saying, "I can't, I just have to go to the washroom."

After a few hours, my mother shouted at my father, "When will you finish your prayers? You started two hours ago. Then you'll tell me that you're getting late for office."

My father wound up all his chores, ate his breakfast, took his lunch box and then rode his bicycle to work. His office was about five kilometres away from home.

∞

My mother came to pick us up from the bus stop. The afternoon sun was very hot and scorching and she always carried a water bottle filled with cool hand pump water. We quenched our thirst with this fresh and cold water. Once we were home, it was my mother's task to handle naughty Priyanshu. We generally sat on the floor of our bedroom to eat the tasty lunch prepared by my mother. The grey floor was cool and we enjoyed sitting on the floor especially during the summer months. My mother drew the yellow, white and red vertical striped curtains to keep the sun out. Looking at the curtains, anyone would be able to guess our middle class status. My mother had bought it from a shop on instalments. Big pink and red spots were visible on it. These spots had been created by me. Whenever my mother went out, I applied her sticky dark lip shades on my lips, wrapped myself in a dupatta and looked in the mirror to see how I would look when I grew up to be a young woman. When the main door opened with a bang, it was a signal that my mother had arrived. I would wipe my lips on the curtains, quickly remove the dupatta and get back to my books to show that I was a really studious child who didn't have a life beyond her books.

The ceiling fan whirred at its maximum speed making me feel sleepy in the cruel summer heat. Priyanshu was still pestering my mother with his demands, "Mom, I need a new pencil box. I've lost the old one. Mom, I need a new lunch box too." My mother told him to keep quiet. He, however, started crying again. This irritated her a lot and finally her patience gave way. Another round of slaps made his cheeks turn red. After a few minutes, he finally stopped crying. Then Mother told us to sleep for two hours and to do our homework after that.

We woke up after the two hours had passed. I, being a perfect book worm, opened my books and started doing my homework while Priyanshu ran out to play cricket or marbles with the children in the colony.

In the evening, when my father came back and started ringing the doorbell impatiently as usual, everyone in the family reset their respective positions, just like a driver driving without a seat belt tries to pull the seat belt across himself on seeing the traffic police. All my uncles and aunts would get back to their study tables to show my father that they were sincere scholars and each one would tell the other to be serious as my father (their eldest brother) had arrived.

Father started with his list of questions as soon as he entered home, "Where's Priyanshu? Where is Naina? What are the others doing?"

This was the cue for my mother to start with her list of complaints. And if there was a complaint against Priyanshu and me (from anyone in the family) then we were punished. I was over-sensitive, but at the same time, if I made a mistake I would accept it. But for Priyanshu, it was just a joke every evening. He never took all this seriously until my father slapped him a few times. I remember that even after being punished, he used to give me an impish smile and then we would go through our lessons before going to bed.

> Our family had limited means. We did not have any luxury items like refrigerators, televisions and air conditioners. While other people watched family shows on their television sets, we would entertain ourselves with our little joint family fights over stupid issues.

Sometimes, father came home early in the evening. He gave us a ride on his bicycle and took us straight to the street vendors where we enjoyed mouthwatering aloo tikkis and matka kulfi (a local version of delicious homemade ice cream). We always felt extremely happy on that day. My father never took us to any restaurants for family dinners because it was beyond his budget. We did not have the custom of cutting birthday cakes - birthdays were always celebrated by offering prayers at the temple and having family get-togethers at home. We constantly longed for invitations where we would get a chance to attend the cake cutting ceremony and relish creamy birthday cakes.

∞

My father had to leave his job because of health reasons. He started taking tuitions and this became the only source of income for us. The proverb - as you sow so you reap - aptly described my father's situation. He worked so hard that within a short span of time, he became a renowned tutor in Yamuna Nagar. Many prominent people in our town started calling him to coach their children for entrance examinations. His students performed well in these examinations and got selected in various colleges. My father became the most sought after tutor of Yamuna Nagar. His tutorials helped many poor students also.

As our financial condition improved a little, Father thought of replacing his bicycle with a scooty. This was the first time that we saw our father progress in life and we were all happy with his accomplishments. Priyanshu, however, had his own reasons for feeling happy as he planned to use it to ride to school. But what poor Priyanshu did not understand was that my father would never allow a naughty boy like him to use his scooty knowing full well that his son would make the scooty fly on the roads of Yamuna Nagar.

Whenever my father received a wedding invitation from any of his colleagues, he would take all of us on his scooty to the wedding. My mother and Priyanshu would be accommodated on the back seat while I would share the space on the front seat with my father. We always looked enviously at the families who came in their cars and parked them alongside the venue. My father would proudly park his scooty along with these cars but we always felt inferior because we had only a two wheeler instead of a four wheeler.

It was difficult for my father to buy a car because our education and other family expenses were enough to drain all the money out of his pockets. With our limited means, it seemed sinful to aspire for bigger things.

One fine day, my father took us to his student's birthday party. The boy was the son of an industrialist. Priyanshu and I wore our best party clothes. The venue was a plush bungalow with a lawn. My father parked his scooty along with the cars and once again, we noticed that our scooty was the only two wheeler in the parking area. The others had come in their big expensive cars.

Priyanshu and I got down from the scooty and looked at the bungalow. It was very beautiful, and seemed out of a Hindi movie. We entered the house and were spellbound by the luxurious, spacious and designed-to-perfection interiors. The party had been organised on a big, lush, green lawn with a swing and a cane sofa in one corner. There were servants' quarters and a garage at the end of the lawn. Invitees had come from different parts of the town. Ladies dressed in expensive saris were chit chatting with each other holding colourful drinks in their hands. There was a group of children who were dressed in expensive dresses. There were six or seven servants running here and there, busy serving all the guests. Priyanshu and I felt awkward as we had never seen such a life. We did not know that a birthday party could be so lavish. We looked at the rich people's children and couldn't muster enough strength to join them. A young girl greeted my father and welcomed him. She even asked us to join in the games. We enjoyed playing tambola and musical chairs with the other children.

In my heart I often wondered why we couldn't live such a life. Why should our lives be any different from the lives of these children? Why should these ladies have expensive saris while my mother wore only simple saris? How could parents spend so much on the birthday celebrations of their son, while in my family, we didn't have the means to do so? So many questions were running through my head. Once again, they were left unanswered and I could only sigh in bewilderment.

It was now time to cut the cake and everyone gathered at one place. Priyanshu and I hastily left our chairs and reached the table. The birthday boy cut the guitar shaped cake and the waiters served it to all the guests.

We got one slice each of the cake but unfortunately, it was not as big as we had expected it to be. We were hesitant to ask for a bigger portion of the cake because our parents had always taught us to behave appropriately whenever we were at someone else's place.

Dinner was served after this. There was a variety of items including snacks, drinks, dishes of chicken, mutton, paneer, desserts and so on and so forth. The list was endless.

When my mother was not around, my father always made sure he used every opportunity he got to enjoy drinks. He escaped to a corner to enjoy his glass of wine.

It was almost midnight and now it was time to leave for home.

> I have great parents who have spent beyond their means to give us the best lifestyle they could afford. I remember our financial position was not always comfortable and often we had to wait for things. My mother knew how to manage her household budget. She always thought about her children, her husband and then about herself. Whenever we wanted to buy new clothes, we would put our demands in front of our

mother. She would share it with my father and then both of them would tell us, "This month it's not possible but from the next month's salary we'll buy you clothes."

My parents would start preparing the budget for the following month. It included our school fees, household expenses, contribution to the education expenses of my uncles and aunts, monthly savings and much more ....

Somewhere in this tight budget, they would fit in the requirements of their children by cutting down a few of their own expenses and this cut down usually took place on my mother's expenses. She hardly bought two saris a year for her everyday use.

Every summer vacation we used to visit our maternal grandmother and uncles. This was the only time when we didn't have to follow our father's strict regime. We would enjoy during the day as well as in the night, as there was no one to wake us up early in the morning to teach us lessons or ask us to go to bed early. That's why we always liked our summer holidays the most. But our father, being the way he was, would put forward a non-negotiable condition in front of us, "First you'll have to finish your holiday homework within fifteen days without putting it off. Only after that will I allow you to leave for your grandmother's place." I always finished my holiday homework very quickly but as usual, Priyanshu would do it at the eleventh hour.

My father could be a perfect finance minister if he ever wanted to be. He planned his expenses in such a way that my mother was able to visit her mother's place and also buy gifts for her family. It was only after we had met our deadlines as scheduled by my father that we could start preparing for this journey.

Mother had a habit of carrying a lot of luggage. One special bag would always be packed with things to eat because my father was very fond of food but he would never buy anything from vendors at railway stations. That bag would be full of spoons, glasses, a knife, black salt, paper plates, biscuits, twenty to thirty puris, two curries, cucumber, pickles, lemons, green chillies, red onions and a lot more. Whenever a vendor came to sell food items in the train, Priyanshu and I would wink at my mother and tell her to buy something from him. But who could convince my father? He would tell us, "Kids, do not buy these items as they are not hygienic and in any case, nothing is better than homemade food." That would be the end of our desire and we would silently say goodbye to that vendor.

It was a very long and excruciating journey from Ambala to Etawah but for us, it was full of excitement as though we were going for an exotic vacation. The train stopped at nearly twenty five stations.

It was very hot in June but we inevitably had to travel in the general compartment because my father could not afford tickets in the AC class. Lucky are those who have money to travel in comfort. For us it was a dream to travel by air conditioned coach but we did not know when it would be fulfilled.

The longest stopover was at the New Delhi railway station. When the train arrived at New Delhi, I peeped out of the window and looked at the people who were hurriedly going here and there. Whenever I looked at the crowd in Delhi, I always felt envious of the fact that people in big cities were so different from those who belonged to small towns. "How come this metropolis crowd is so smart, both in their looks and communication skills," I wondered. "Will we ever become a part of them?"

While so many thoughts were running through my mind, Priyanshu and Mother were busy sleeping - they were the sort who could easily miss their station because of their sleep. They always needed someone to wake them up before time and it was my father and I who had to deal with it.

My father was very talkative and he had acquired knowledge on a number of topics which he loved to share with people. He also loved to give suggestions freely. Sometimes, it was irritating for us, as we never understood how someone could give advice without bothering to find out whether the others liked it or not.

In the general class, there was usually a group of people who would misbehave especially with women. Most of the miscreants could be seen staring at ladies or even physically harassing women and girls. As the train crossed one station after another, it became even more crowded. I thought hopelessly, "In a country like India where there is a huge population explosion, it is normal to find so many people travelling in a train's general compartment. And naturally, every- one thinks they can fit in just about anywhere." In the general compartment, people could be seen sitting in every corner - on the floor, under the seats, near the toilets. At night if someone wanted to go to the toilet, they would have great difficulty walking from their seat to the toilet. A few of them played cards while another set of passengers fought for seats. I do not know why people are always ready to fight on minor issues that can otherwise be resolved with a little maturity.

Every compartment had an alarm chain for emergencies but this became a boon only for thieves and villagers who travelled without tickets, as they could stop the train in the middle of the jungle and jump off without getting caught. This would happen twice or thrice in the night.

I never used the train's toilet because of the unhygienic and filthy conditions which always made me want to throw up. I often wondered if I ever would get a chance to travel in the AC class.

It was three in the morning and the train was about to reach Etawah station. My father tried to wake up my mother and Priyanshu but they only managed to get up and walk to the door drowsily after quite a while.

We got off at the station and felt a sense of exhilaration. We took a bus from Etawah to the small village of Lakhna and reached my grandmother's place. In villages, people generally get up early. It was only six in the morning and people could be seen milking cows, brushing their teeth with neem twigs or even bathing near wells. Whenever I looked at them, I got the feeling that even though they did not have a high standard of living yet they seemed to be satisfied with their lives.

When we entered my grandmother's house, everyone in the vicinity started talking amongst themselves, "Dolly has come with her kids. Look at her daughter, she is so beautiful and she resembles her mother. Look, look at little Priyanshu, he's still in his half pants."

Priyanshu had a lot of friends who were of his age group. They always used to tease him and make fun of him, "Hey, your half pants are so loose……", and with that, they would probably threaten to pull them down!

Grandmother looked at us with tears of happiness in her eyes. She was overjoyed to see us. She would wait throughout the year for this moment. She hugged us tightly and smothered us with kisses. We escaped from her arms and went upstairs to meet our two uncles who were still sleeping blissfully on the terrace. We jumped onto them making them wake up in shock but once they realised it was us, their happiness knew no bounds. "The moment you enter Grandma's place, you start disturbing everyone in Lakhna!" To which we replied, "Uncle, get up and go to the market and bring some hot jalebis for us." In villages, jalebis are often eaten at breakfast time. Our uncles were so happy to see us, they were willing to go to any lengths to fulfil our wishes.

Our maternal grandmother's house was different from our house in Yamuna Nagar. Here people did not have electricity, so our grandmother used to make oil lamps from ink pots. She would fill them with kerosene oil and dip wicks in them and light them as lamps. This was the only source of light in their rooms and in the kitchen. As they did not have ceiling fans, after sunset, the uncles would throw two or three buckets of water on the terrace to cool it and bring down the temperature and everyone would sleep on stringed cots there. Grandmother had a well in her house from which she would draw water that was sweet and cold. In the rainy season, she poured some medicine into it to make the water potable.

Another interesting fact was that Lakhna faced the menace of monkeys that made everyone's life difficult especially when the monkeys were hungry. I remember a funny incident. It was a sunny afternoon and my mother was washing our clothes near the well and hanging them on the clothesline in the big, open veranda. The monkeys came and took away my father's underwear. It was rather large in size and had colourful stripes on it. My grandmother noticed this from her kitchen window and started shouting, "Dolly, bring a stick and frighten these monkeys. They are tearing your husband's underclothes." My mother came out running like a warrior. She tried to scare them but it was of no use as the monkeys were determined not to give up and instead, started scaring her by clenching their teeth. Mother had enough presence of mind to throw tiny packets containing handfuls of rice and wheat in front of them. Having got what they wanted, the monkeys left that undergarment. Grandmother looked at the torn undergarment and told my mother in all seriousness, "Well, it's in such a condition that I can't repair it but I can sew your kid's underwear out of it."

My father was respected a lot at his in-law's place. In India, the daughter's husband is treated like a God. My grandmother would spend her whole day in front of the mud stove to cook delicious and special food for my father. After dropping us there, my father returned to Yamuna Nagar after two days.

Every morning Priyanshu and I would get up at seven o'clock to enjoy the hot bed tea made by our grandmother and we would always ask our uncles to bring us snacks like pakoras, kachoris etc., from the market.

Vipul lived in my grandmother's neighbourhood and he and Priyanshu were good friends. He had two sisters called Tinky and Dinky. Their uncle Vijay was a vendor who used to sell aloo chaat and was blessed with three daughters – Reena, Meena and Sheena. Vipul's family had children of almost every size and age and every year, either Vipul's mother or his aunt would be expecting a baby. Vipul's mother was obese and his father was a shopkeeper who had a small business. I have seen that man slog all day long and he made decent profits from his business.

Every day Vipul and Priyanshu would borrow Chacha Chaudhary, Pinki and Nandan comics from a small lending library at fifty paisa per comic book. Otherwise, the two boys would roam around the whole village of Lakhna. They would venture into fields which were on the outskirts, go to the Queen's palace or to Vijay's stall to eat aloo chaat for free. Everyone in Lakhna market knew Priyanshu very well. Every shopkeeper greeted him warmly as they thought that Priyanshu and I lived in a city which was far better than their village of Lakhna. They would ask him, "Hey do you study in an English school?" To which Priyanshu would reply in English and leave the poor villagers further spellbound. We made a great impression on them as they always thought that we were better than them.

Priyanshu had another friend named Mallu. Mallu never went to school. His father had gotten married twice. Everyone in the village used to tease him, "Hey Mallu, how is your second Mom? What she is doing at home with your father? Come on, tell us."

There was something odd about the children in my grandmother's neighbourhood – none of them were properly clad in summer. They bathed several times a day at the well situated in the corner of the street and ran around Lakhna only in their underclothes.

I too had a couple of friends in Lakhna with whom I would play the whole day. Everyone would bring their dolls and then we would get our dolls married. My friends Dinky and Tinky were very naughty. They knew all the gossip about the Lakhna inhabitants. Every evening, Priyanshu, Tinky, Dinky, Vipul and I would sit on the porch in front of Vipul's house and make fun of every passerby.

At night everyone came back home for dinner which my grandmother and mother had cooked for us. All of us sat on the floor to have a candle lit dinner which was in reality, by the light of a kerosene lamp. After dinner, we would keep sitting at the same place for two hours, as my uncles had a lot of gossip to share. Sometimes, after dinner, my grandmother would talk with Priyanshu and me about her past. "You know, your grandfather died of asthma when your mother was only nineteen years old and your uncles were very young. I had no one to help me with the children's education. I earned money by selling milk. When your mother entered her teens, I had to get her married with the help of my relatives. Your youngest uncle's hobby is painting. He paints posters and banners for shop-keepers and gets paid. This is the only source of income for us."

> I have come to realise that every one's life revolves around problems. Our own problems appear small when we listen to the problems faced by others.

One month passed happily with our friends and the monkeys which would visit us from time to time. Soon, it was time to leave Lakhna and go back to Yamuna Nagar. My grandmother and my uncles were very sad as they would have to wait for one more year before they saw us again. Grandmother always sent us back with double the luggage we had brought with us. She packed homemade snacks, pickles and many other eatables for us. These eatables would last for one whole year.

We boarded the train from Etawah to Ambala. After a night's journey, the train reached Ambala Cantt. station. Father came to pick us up. He was delighted to see us, and in an attempt to be funny, insisted on making wisecracks, "Hey, why is your luggage so heavy? I think you have stuffed stones and bricks in it. How will I pick it up?"

We took a bus from Ambala to Yamuna Nagar. Priyanshu and I missed our maternal grandmother's house very badly. However, after reaching Yamuna Nagar, within a few days, we went back to our routine life.

After a few years, my father joined a new office as tuitions were not providing us with financial stability. A year later, his salary increased and my father planned to buy a room cooler to beat the heat and sleep peacefully at night. My mother told us about my father's plans and Priyanshu and I were thrilled to hear this. "Wow Mom, this means that from now on, we'll have chilled drinking water at home just like at school where we have so many water coolers!" My mother laughed and told me, "No sweetheart, this isn't a water cooler. It's a room cooler which runs on electricity and water. You'll see when your father brings it."

Soon it was the weekend that we were desperately waiting for. My father brought home a room cooler. Priyanshu and I looked at it in wonder. It was a big metal box which had a big water tank, a motor and an exhaust fan fitted in it. When it was switched on, the motor drew water from the tank and sprinkled it on the wood wool pads on the walls of the cooler and wet them. As the fan rotated at a high speed, it sucked the air across the wet pads and within a few minutes, the temperature of the room was considerably lower. I covered myself with a blanket as I had started sneezing. Mother laughed and said "You're feeling cold because you aren't used to a room cooler. Don't worry, you'll get used to it within a few days."

Priyanshu and I felt we had at last become rich and boasted about our new room cooler at school. But the other children told us that they already had room coolers in their homes and it was nothing new for them. For Priyanshu and me, it was something new as we had always slept under a ceiling fan.

Within a few months, our final exams started. I was in the fourth standard while Priyanshu was in the third standard. We got the date sheet for our exams and saw that we had two days of preparatory leave before each exam. My father looked at the date sheet and planned his work accordingly so that he could help us prepare for the exams. He would wake us up at four every morning and sometimes, he took us to his workplace where he taught us our lessons while doing his work alongside. Father always worked hard with us during our exam days.

After our exams were over, he received an invitation letter to attend the parent teacher meeting. He visited our school and met all the teachers.

All of them were impressed with my father and understood that he took pains for his children's study. He received the report cards and felt happy as I had stood second and Priyanshu had stood first in class. Father returned home with sweets and told everyone in the house the good news. He encouraged me to get the first position in future.

"Keep it up," he said. "I have so many dreams for you and I want to see both of you well settled in your lives. My life is for you kids, it doesn't matter how much I have to cut down on my expenses. I am saving money for your education only. I want to see both of you always on the top."

My mother told us, "You should be ambitious and put in your best to attain your goals. This is just the first step towards success."

My grandmother was elated about Priyanshu's result, "Look at my grandson, Priyanshu. He is just brilliant! That's the reason he comes first in class even though he is not a bookworm like Naina. Mark my words, Priyanshu will be an engineer one day. As for Naina, it will be wiser to marry her off after her graduation."

> I was very unhappy listening to my grandmother's sarcasm which was so typical of her. Sometimes, such taunting words drive you to achieve the impossible and lay a strong foundation for your goals. However, I do not have any hard feelings towards my grandmother because she was born and brought up in an environment where boys were considered to be the superior beings and the driving force of a family. She taught her children - my uncles and my father - to fight against odds and achieve something in their lives. She is not among us now and we miss her for the sacrifices she made for our family.

A few days later, we joined our new classes. My father had to arrange for money for our books and admission fees. "Dolly, this year the school fees are higher and the books are also very expensive. We need to see how we can manage with my salary. Expenses are so high that it is becoming difficult to survive. How can one meet all the expenditures on a single person's earnings?"

Mother was upset and shouted at my father, "Look, I wanted to take up a job after I got married but your family did not support me. Everyone wanted me to take care of your house and the children. Tell me, would it have been feasible for me to do all this along with a job? Now, let bygones be bygones and think about the present and the future." She controlled her anger and after taking a deep breath said, "Please don't worry. I save some money every month from your salary. You can utilise it for the children now. She opened her almirah, took out her big purse, in which there was a small purse and within that small purse, there was yet another tiny purse! She finally took out money from her secret purse and gave it to my father. "You are a very smart housewife and I like this quality of yours," my father said to please my mother. "You don't have to flatter me", she countered, "now you can go and pay the school fees."

When my father had left for our school, Mother murmured, 'Does he know about all my savings? I've kept some money in the rice container and I want to use it to buy new clothes for my kids on Diwali. They will be happy and I'm happy when they're happy."

A few months later on the day of Holi, Priyanshu and I asked for my father's and uncle's permission to go out and celebrate the festival of colours with our friends. But neither of them allowed us. "In our family no one plays with colours as we don't like it. Don't you dare go out to play." We felt sad and peeped out of the window. We saw everyone smeared with colours and enjoying every single moment of Holi dancing to the beats of the Punjabi dhol.

I was furious and asked Priyanshu, "Why do you think our family is so conservative? They have never enjoyed in their lives and want us to live our lives the same way. Priyanshu said, "I'm going onto the roof top and from there I will jump onto the neighbour's roof and play with my friends there. But you should stay here only as you're a girl and no one will forgive you if you come with me to play. Even Priyanshu at his young age understood and believed in the behaviour expected of girls on such a day.

My brother ran off and came back after two hours looking like a black sheep. My father looked at him and lost his temper. He ordered him to take a bath and come back with his books. For my father, studies were more important than any other activity in life. There was not a single day when he did not teach us or supervise our studies, including festivals and holidays.

We celebrated Diwali a few months later. Everyone got up in the morning and wished each other "Happy Diwali". My mother made a list of sweets to be bought and gave it to my father, who dutifully went to his favourite sweet shop to buy the sweets. He asked the shopkeeper to let him sample all the sweets on the list and then he bought what he thought were the best ones. He returned home and took all of us – my grandmother, my mother and both of us to Meena Bazaar, which was one of the most famous markets in Yamuna Nagar. Mother bought new clothes for us, while my grandmother bought earthenware lamps, candles, statues of Lakshmi, the goddess of wealth and Ganesh, the lord of success. She also bought yellow marigold flowers for the puja in the evening. Priyanshu and I scanned the market and asked our father to buy us some crackers. He refused, "I won't buy you crackers because they may cause accidents. Also, I don't have money to waste on crackers."

We returned home and opened the gifts that my father had received from his old students. There were some expensive sweets and good quality dinner sets. I said, "Wow Mom! These must be very expensive. Rich people have so much money to spend." My father said, "They are big people. You know Naina, they buy crackers for five to ten thousand rupees every Diwali." I thought to myself, "God, when will we be able to buy such expensive things and spend this kind of money on crackers?"

A few years later, my third uncle Sanjay got a job as a Chemistry teacher. He was offered a decent pay package. He also started taking extra classes and earned a reasonably good amount of money. One fine day he bought a refrigerator for the house. Everyone was very happy and Priyanshu and I were thankful, "Now we have one more luxury item at home. When we come back from school, we'll drink chilled water and cold milk."

Within a few months, Sanjay Uncle bought a piece of land in which to construct his own house. Our family was large and it was becoming increasingly difficult to live in a three bedroom house. My father supported his brother's decision.

Some months later, the construction work was completed. Now there was just one wall between the old house and the new house. The whole family including our grandmother, uncles and aunts shifted to the new house except for Uncle Nagendra and my father who stayed back in the old house with their respective families. This old house had been constructed by my father a long time ago. He was the first one in the family to have constructed his own house. He had taken a loan from the bank and had paid back instalments every month out of his salary.

As time passed, Priyanshu and I grew old enough to understand the nuances of life but in no way did our mischievous nature lessen with age. Now our mother did not come to pick us up from the bus stop any more. We returned home from the bus stop by ourselves. One day when we were on our way home, Priyanshu started teasing me, "I will break your doll's house and your doll will not live to see another day." I was furious with him and pushed him hard. Priyanshu fell over a heap of cow dung on the road. His white school uniform was stained badly with dung and he smelt very bad. He fumed, "Just you wait, I'll tell Dad and Mom and they'll teach you a lesson."

On reaching home, Priyanshu narrated the whole incident to my mother after a lot of exaggeration. My mother slapped me hard. Priyanshu was happy and he stopped crying. We did not talk to each other for a few hours but after some time, we actually forgot everything and started talking to each other once again.

A few days later my father disclosed to my mother, "I am thinking of buying a black and white television." My mother asked anxiously, "Have you asked about the cost of a new television?" My father said, "I haven't, but I'll go to an electronics shop and enquire about it."

The next day he came back and told my mother that a new TV was very expensive and would cost approximately three thousand rupees, which was why he was considering buying a second hand television. He felt it wasn't necessary to buy only new things.

The following week he bought a second hand television for a thousand rupees at a monthly instalment of a hundred rupees. We watched television for the first time at home and felt very happy. Every afternoon, after coming back from school, we would watch our favourite television programmes - Puppet Shows, Small Wonder and Mowgli, among others.

We told our friends in school that we had bought a black and white television. Our friends told us that they had colour television sets at home which were better than black and white television sets. Priyanshu and I came back home disheartened and asked why our father hadn't bought a colour television set. Our mother patiently explained that we couldn't afford a colour TV because they were very expensive.

Mother was concerned about Priyanshu because he would watch television all the time and ignore his studies. She complained to my father who shouted at Priyanshu and kept the television inside an old wooden cabinet and locked it. He gave the keys to my mother and scolded Priyanshu, "Your exams start next month. Concentrate on your studies. Don't you dare break the rules!"

Priyanshu was a born engineer and knew now he would never get to see his favourite shows in the afternoon. He thought about it and when my mother was tired and had fallen sleep in the afternoon, he used a thin aluminum wire to open the lock. When my mother got up, he switched off the television and closed the television cabinet.

One evening, when my father came back from office, he noticed some scratches on the cabinet. He called Priyanshu and asked him if he had tried to open the cabinet lock with a piece of wire. Priyanshu refused to admit he had anything to do with it.

Dad shouted at him and slapped him. "Don't you ever lie to me. I work from morning to night to give you a better life. I'm doing everything possible to get you settled. I'm saving money for your higher studies, doing overtime without enjoying my own life. But you, you are ignoring your studies." He also yelled at my mother, "What kind of a mother are you? You don't know what your kids do when you're asleep. Whenever I come back home after a tough day, I have to solve all your problems. What kind of life am I living? I should leave this house. I'll go and live somewhere else and none of you will ever find me."

Mother, Priyanshu and I started crying after all this mess. My father opened the main gate and left home in frustration. My mother started sobbing and we were horrified. My grandmother came to console us, "Don't worry, he'll come back."

Indeed, my father did come back after half an hour! He did not talk to anyone, just took a bath and said his prayers. At night my mother asked us to apologise to him. He then talked to us calmly, "I cannot run away from my responsibilities. But you should co-operate with me as I am doing all this for your good only." We both apologised to him and went to bed. The following day we woke up together as a family and a new day began.

Some months later, my eldest aunt Neeta passed her M.A. (English) examination with distinction. She wanted to be independent, so she started looking for a job as a school teacher. Soon she got a call for an interview from a government school and happily told everyone in the family about it.

My uncle Sanjay, being very possessive about all the girls in the family, was not happy with her decision. "You won't go out of the house for any job. I won't allow you to travel every day in a local bus to go and teach in some stupid school where you will have male colleagues. What do you want now? I'll give you a fixed amount every month for your survival." She revolted. It was as if someone was trying to shatter her dreams. My father, however, stood by her firmly. "No, she will go and attend the interview," he insisted. "What's wrong if she wants to be an independent girl? I support her decision. No one will stop her!"

The following day, Neeta Aunty woke up at five in the morning and got ready to catch the bus to village Kalanaur. She attended the interview and was selected for the job. She was overjoyed and shared the good news with everyone. From then onwards, she used to get up at five in the morning, get ready, go to school and come back by six in the evening.

One day, she got late while coming back from school. Everyone in the family was worried. Sanjay Uncle lost his temper and shouted at my grandmother, "I told you not to allow her to work. See, she hasn't reached home yet. She is very young and people in this world are bad. We shouldn't allow our girls to lead such lives. She should sit at home and get married as soon as possible."

"Why are you shouting like the devil? She'll come back, perhaps she didn't get the bus on time today," Grandmother shouted back at him.

After one hour, Neeta Aunty came back home and told us that she had not been able to get the bus on time that day. Poor Neeta Aunty! She had to suffer for one hour that day as Sanjay Uncle kept shouting at her.

She decided to change her job so that she wouldn't have to face the same situation in future. She found another job but that was far from home. Therefore, she decided to stay at the women's hostel there and visited home once a month only.

∞

Meanwhile, I completed my primary education. Earlier, Priyanshu and I were studying in the same school, which was from the first to the fifth standard. But for higher education, I had to change my school. At home, everyone discussed which schools were good and would be suitable for me. My other uncles suggested, "Naina is growing up so we shouldn't send her to a co-ed school where boys and girls study together. She should join a girl's school now." My father accordingly sent me to a reputed girl's school where I studied from the sixth standard to the tenth standard.

It felt a little strange on my first day at school, as there were girls everywhere. The teachers were very strict and the girls were not allowed to go out of the school premises from nine in the morning to half past two in the afternoon. There was a canteen in the backyard of the school, which was being run by a young couple. They sold snacks like samosas for one rupee, aloo tikkis and bread pakodas for two rupees each.

For lunch they cooked daal or rajma with rice and sold it at five rupees per plate. Many girls used to bring ten to twenty rupees pocket money every day and enjoyed the canteen food. I also wanted to try all the mouth-watering dishes. My mother used to give me five rupees every three days. I utilised the money to pay the auto rickshaw while going back home from school.

One day I asked my mother to give me more pocket money but she said, "My dear child, we can't afford to give you more than this as we have to manage everything in your father's salary. I'll cook everything for you at home, then you won't feel like eating outside food. Moreover, you carry your lunch box every day. If we overspend like this, things will become difficult for us." I was disheartened and asked God, "Lord, when will you change our days so that we can eat anything anywhere and there aren't any limitations in life?"

With time, I realised that girls in co-ed schools are better groomed than girls in an all girls' school. I discussed this with my family but no one agreed with me. It was difficult to have open discussions because ours was a conservative family. Thus, I found it extremely difficult to convince them about the way I felt.

My father, meanwhile, was gradually progressing in life. A few months later, Dad finished paying instalments for the television. He now wanted to buy a two wheeler so that his grown up children could ride comfortably. He told everyone in the family, "I will buy it on instalments." I was excited, "Dad, I will choose the colour for you. You always say I am your adorable daughter!" My father agreed readily, "Yes my dear, I'll buy a scooter of your choice." The following week Father and I visited a two wheeler showroom. There were twenty scooters standing in a row. They were in different colours. One well-dressed boy came forward. He was wearing a white shirt and black trousers. He tried to be the perfect salesman but I found there was a bad odour coming from him as if he hadn't bathed or changed his clothes.

"Welcome Sir, please tell me which colour you would like to select." "It will be my daughter's choice," my father replied. The salesman came closer to me and whispered in my ears, "Come on Sweety, choose one for your Dad." Salesmen in general are sweet tongued people - they know how to use their smiles, their body language and their communication skills to sell almost anything in this world. They give you the impression that you are the most deserving person on this earth.

My husband, who also drives the sales in his organisation, nodded his head in acknowledgement when I narrated this to him.

In just one minute I had scanned all the scooters kept in a row in the showroom. They were so well arranged in one room, it reminded me of my mother arranging our clothes in our small almirah. I put my little finger on a light brown scooter. My father, standing at the far end of the room, said loudly, "Even I wanted that one. Good choice!"

"Ok Sir, so your daughter has finalised this deal. Come with me and we'll finish all the paper work and then the scooter will be yours," the salesman appeared to be grateful. It seemed we had helped him meet his sales target. In one hour we had finished all the formalities. My father gave me the first ride on his scooter. While driving, we talked to each other, "First we'll buy sweets and then we'll go to the temple to thank God for giving us this happiness."

After visiting the temple, we returned home. Dad parked the scooter outside the house. On hearing the scooter's horn, everyone in the neighbourhood came out of their houses to see our new scooter. One aunty looked at the new scooter and said, "Have you bought a new scooter? Congratulations!" She called her four children, "Look, Uncle has bought a new scooter!" Small children who were not fully clad came to look at the scooter. One wiped his nose clumsily and smiled at my father. I found it to be very funny. This aunty was an informer par excellence for the entire colony, as she always knew what was brewing in all the households. Now, everyone in the whole colony would know about it. I rang the doorbell and my mother came running out and opened the door. Priyanshu and Mother looked at the scooter and smiled. Priyanshu ate the sweets we had bought and said, "Dad, now I will take your scooty as you don't need it. I will go to school on the scooty as all my friends have their own vehicles." My father replied like an angry commander, "No, you can't drive until you get a license."

My father started dropping us to our respective schools on his new scooter every day. But the ride on the scooter wasn't comfortable enough, as he always took one half of the seat and asked us to adjust on the other half. Whenever we asked my father to shift forward he replied, "Look, I am driving so I should be in a comfortable position. If I sit on the edge of the seat then how will I drive and apply the foot brake. It's only you people who don't know anything about adjustments." We whispered behind his back, "Dad cannot adjust with the two of us, then how will four of us adjust on this new scooter? As usual, when we go somewhere together, Mom will have to come by auto rickshaw."

Two years later, when I was in the eighth standard, Dad got a telephone connection at home. Phone connections were very expensive at that time. Dad could afford all the free incoming calls but only a few important outgoing calls. He gave his phone number to his family and friends but rapidly it reached our neighbours also. Now, every second day, we started receiving calls even for people who lived two kilometres away from our house. In a few months, we started feeling as if we had opened a public telephone booth. Telephone numbers are like fire which rapidly spread everywhere.

There was a boys' school near my school. Whenever girls came out of the school, the boys would gather there just to look at the beautiful girls. Some miscreants also tried to eve tease the girls and misbehave with them.

There is one problem in small cities; often, there are about a hundred boys chasing one beautiful girl as they do not have many options in a small city. Some days later, my mother complained to my father about some blank calls.. Everyone suspected that these calls were for me while I did not even know who was calling and for what? People in conservative families tend to make issues out of every small matter.

I passed my matriculation examination from the girls' school. After this, everyone in my family got together to decide what I should study further. No one even asked me once what I wished to do. I just had to adhere to their decisions. After a collective decision had been taken, I was told to go in for the non-medical stream – with Physics, Chemistry and Maths. I had to change my school also, as this option was not available in my current school. Again, everyone in the family sat down to decide where I should study. Sanjay Uncle's school was chosen for me so that I could study under my uncle's supervision. This was a co-ed school.

> Sanjay Uncle was a tough man from outside but he was so clean hearted and soft from inside. He always helped me and Priyanshu in our studies. I am so thankful to him.

I knew that now my life would become tougher as every action of mine would be monitored by my uncle. He told me before I joined the school itself, "There is no dress code for the eleventh and the twelfth standard, so you'll wear only salwar kameez with no deep necks. Jeans and T shirts are not allowed."

This is a problem that girls in small cities face. A girl's life ends before it actually begins. This was happening with me also. Every day that I had lived, I had lived a life full of restrictions. But now, I was about to take the first step towards my liberation.

3
As a Young Girl

By the age of sixteen, I had grown up to be a fair, tall and well-built girl. The mirror complimented me, in it I could see a girl with beautiful eyes and a tiny nose on a lovely face, and long silky black hair I was often appreciated for my beauty and simplicity.. In the new school, many boys were attracted to me on the first day itself but no one knew that I was their teacher's niece. Some of them had also enquired about my name and telephone number. Hardly one week had passed when I was told that a boy from another class had started following me. I had also noticed him sometimes and I wondered whether he was actually following me or it was just idle gossip.

I can't forget the first love letter that I received. One day, I was sitting in the classroom with my friends and we were busy gossiping. Suddenly, the same boy came near my seat, placed a letter quietly under my palm on the bench and left the class. I had never faced such a weird situation in my life. I was so scared that I started sweating profusely. So much so that I even started shivering and didn't know what to do. I told my friends what had happened and all of us went to the common room and read the letter. My friends laughed when they read the letter which was written in very dramatic language and had many hearts drawn on it.

> Today when I narrate those lines to my husband, he teases me, "God has been so kind to the poor guy and saved his life. Look at me, I haven't been so lucky!"

Now, years later, I can joke about it but at that time, my face turned pale in fear. If my uncle got to know about it, he would definitely blame me for everything even though we all knew that it wasn't my fault. In my family, no one would think for a moment that I was innocent. Instead, they might even imagine that I had triggered it all.

My friends suggested that I show this letter to my uncle so that he would know that I was innocent. I went to look for him in the school laboratory but unfortunately, he wasn't there at that time. I didn't want to lose a moment to prove my innocence. My friends advised me to tell the head master. I narrated the whole incident to him. He took the letter from my hands and assured me that he would take action against that boy.

I was so scared that I left school after half day and went back home. I didn't know what was going to happen. My mother was engrossed in her 'Saas bahu' serial on television about mothers-in-law and daughters-in-law. She asked me why I had returned so early. "I wasn't feeling well so I came back," I replied.

After a few hours, my uncle came home and by that time, he was well aware of the whole incident. He started shouting at me, "Naina, I know you are innocent but who will believe me? Everyone in school will wonder why only you are being chased by boys considering there are many other girls in the school also. I can't tolerate the fact that someone dares to give a love letter to our daughter. I had already said in the beginning that you should be admitted to a girl's school but your father doesn't listen to anyone."

The following day, I came to know from my friends that the trouble maker had been rusticated from school. After this incident, everyone in school came to know that I was 'Sanjay Sir's' niece and even if any boy liked me, none of them dared to approach me.

After some days, one of my friends informed me that there was a back bencher who used to stare at me. Apparently he liked me, but being scared of my uncle, he didn't want to make any effort to disclose it to me. Sometimes, I caught a glimpse of him staring at me. He seemed to be a very serious person. It was clear that he couldn't mask his feelings - it was clearly visible in his eyes. He might have been drawn towards me but I ignored him and never spoke to him about all this. One day in class, everyone was in the mood to have fun. Each one came forward with jokes, songs or skits to entertain the class. This fellow didn't want to miss this golden opportunity to express his feelings for me, albeit indirectly. He came forward and sang a Hindi movie song.

My friends and I could easily make out that he was singing for me. All my friends laughed and I felt awkward.

Within those two years in school, I had to live my life according to the strict instructions of my uncle and my family. As a result, I never wore skirts, T shirts or trousers. I was only allowed to wear salwar kameez and I was never allowed to go anywhere after my school hours.

I completed two years in that school. On my last day of school I felt a little better. It was as if I had come out of a prison. My father asked me to attend coaching classes in Yamuna Nagar itself to prepare for the engineering entrance examination. I knew that it would be difficult for me to clear the test as I had never understood the concepts of chemistry and physics although I was good at mathematics. My father spent a lot of money on my coaching and entrance exams.

After one month I got my results. I hadn't cleared my exams. My parents were very upset and my father yelled at me, "You've failed and brought shame to us. All my colleagues have children your age and all of them have cleared the entrance exams. They will get admission in good colleges and will settle down. What will I say to them when they bring sweets to celebrate their success?"

On hearing these harsh words, I was discouraged and cried for hours as I hadn't been able to make my father proud of me. He returned in the evening and talked to me calmly, "Naina, whatever has been done can't be undone; now you should apply in some local college for graduation." Once again, there were discussions at home about which stream I should take for my graduation - science or arts.

All my uncles wished that I should aim to become a teacher as it was the preferred option for most people in the family. Moreover, they were well settled in Yamuna Nagar, so I wouldn't be going wrong if I chose a similar career. But this time I stood up for myself. I did not want to follow my family's wishes. I even lost my temper and shouted at my father, "Why should you decide the future of your children according to the wishes of your family members. Will they ever discuss the same thing with you when they have kids? I am not against the teaching profession but I do not want to be a teacher in my life. I have decided that I will study computer science and this time I will not listen to anyone at any cost."

"Why won't you listen to us? We are only thinking about your future," my father insisted.

"Nowadays, there are so many career options but you want me to follow your family's hackneyed way of thinking. I won't become a teacher and that is final," I said rigidly.

After this huge fight between my father and me, he gave in. "Ok fine, I won't force you. But think about it once again."

This time, I intentionally chose a girls' college as I did not want any more problems in life because of boys. I'd had enough of it in the last two years. Being a girls' college, there were one thousand illogical instructions that one had to follow. One of them was that girls can't wear trousers, only salwar kameez.

With time I made a lot of friends in college. There was one Sikh girl named Amrinder Kaur. She was from a rich family. I had a lot of friends in the girls' hostel too. All my hostel friends were from small cities but as they did not live at home, they enjoyed a lot of freedom. There were no restrictions on the hostel girls and they were allowed to wear anything they liked after college hours. They had all kinds of western dresses. I still remember my friends lived in room number 23 in the hostel and I used to spend my free time between lectures over there. It soon became our favourite spot.

All the girls would try each other's dresses, dance, sing and joke with each other. Sometimes, all of us would go out to eat gol gappas in the nearby market. Not only this, a few of my friends were very naughty, they had created four to five email ids and they used to chat using those ids with five different boys at the same time from cyber cafes. One could see multiple chat windows opened simultaneously on their screens. Who would have thought technology would make flirting so easy! Each one of them had boyfriends in every corner of Yamuna Nagar. They would date all of them at different times every Sunday. This was funny and not at all difficult for them. They used to share their boyfriends' stories in room number 23 and it became our favourite pastime.

My hostel friends made it a point to pamper our gate keeper and keep him well-oiled by occasionally giving him some chicken and beer bottles so that he would allow them to go out at any time. They had a lot of fun.

My father, meanwhile, continued to struggle as he required a lot of money for our higher education. He started taking tuitions after office hours so that he could save some extra money for us. However, after some time, he was transferred to Karnal. Now he had to spend four hours extra to travel to his place of work. In any case, his work schedule was very hectic and now it became even more difficult for him to continue with the tuitions that would bring in extra money for our higher education. Every morning he had to get up at five in the morning, bathe and catch a bus to Karnal. In the evening he would come back by seven and then take tuitions till half past ten.

One day, he could not get the bus on the way back to Yamuna Nagar. He was worried about his tuitions and tried to rush and catch the last bus and in his haste, he fell down on the road. He was badly injured and his legs were bruised. People ran to help him and somehow he came back home. When he entered the house, we saw there were big gashes on his arms and he could hardly walk. We were shocked to see him in this condition. It seemed that he was about to cry. He said, "I have to come back on time so that I may not miss any of my tuitions. If I miss any, then my reputation will be at stake and no one will call me to teach their children. Then how will I save money for my children? I was in a hurry and I fell down and hurt myself while running to catch the bus." Tears filled in our eyes and we wanted to cry while he told us about his accident.

∞

I passed my first year of graduation with good marks and this made my father very happy indeed. Now he was sure that I could do something in the field of computers. I was also getting serious about my career. My friends recommended that I should complete my post-graduation from Delhi or Chandigarh as these being big cities had reputed colleges. I was thrilled at the thought of living outside Yamuna Nagar. My friends encouraged me to clear the entrance examination for MCA (Master of Computer Application) and get admission in a good university. I was a different girl now and I had become ambitious.

My father allowed me to join a local computer institute for extra classes for which he had to spend eleven thousand rupees. Gradually, however, I came to realise that such institutes were set up only to fleece students. They made tall claims about providing knowledge and skills, whereas in actuality, they did no such thing. I cautioned my friends against joining any such institute in Yamuna Nagar. My friends, on the other hand, argued that since it was a small city I would perhaps not find any other reputed institute there, but if I joined the same course in Delhi, I would definitely gain a lot. After some days, I left that institute in frustration. I felt guilty that I had wasted my father's hard earned money on a substandard computer institute.

One day I received an anonymous phone call. A stranger whispered to me on the phone, "Naina, I like you and I want to meet you." I asked him who he was and what he wanted. But before he could answer, the phone got disconnected. My mother was listening to all this and asked me, "Who was that guy?" I, of course, denied knowing anything about him. My mother became even more suspicious and started cross questioning me. After a while I told her, "Someone from the computer institute might be chasing me. He must have got my number from somewhere and called me." My mother said, "We'll find out about it and I'll ask your father to drop you to college for some days."

Once again I felt scared as these little issues always stifled my happiness at home. My parents started putting more restrictions on me after this incident and I became a major topic of discussion at home.

Mysteriously enough, till date no one knows who called up and why.

To top it all, we had neighbours who were really pathetic. Sixty percent of the people were illiterate and their standard of living was very low even though they had sufficient money to live a good life. Every day they would exchange sensational gossip about so and so's daughter who had run away with a boy who lived in the next street. The boy happened to be an auto rickshaw driver! Or that a certain lady had applied for divorce as her husband used to drink and beat her every day.

Upon hearing such news, my parents used to feel proud and very righteous about their family. "At least our family is educated and we've earned respect in the eyes of other people irrespective of the fact that we don't have that much money."

> Whenever I saw any metropolis on television, I realised that life in small towns was very slow and different as compared to life in metro cities. I yearned to make a place for myself in a big city and started pursuing my dreams even more seriously.

In Yamuna Nagar, people would get up at five in the morning, bathe, spend a couple of hours on rituals for their Gods and prayers etc., after which they get down to a heavy breakfast of parathas and puris. Shopkeepers would open their shops and start their businesses late in the morning. Middle aged women wearing funny, dark makeup would stand at their main doors to have long gossip sessions.

People had a lot of time to talk about others. If by any chance a girl was seen talking to a boy on the road or in the market, people would say, "Nowadays girls have gone astray, they do not feel ashamed of roaming about openly with a boy. Children these days have ruined our culture."

If any girl wore jeans, boys would ogle at her, whisper about her and laugh at her. If a girl was stylish, she would become the butt of jokes for the boys in college and they would scribble her name on walls along with dirty comments. Girls were rarely seen driving cars. If any girl was seen driving, people would stare at her as if she was an alien who had come down to earth. There is no night life in small cities. Every man is back home by evening and eats dinner with his family.

I wanted to get out of this place very badly. I wanted to see what a big city was like and be part of the life of a metro city. This probably happens to every youngster who lives in a small town.

> Today I live in a big city but at heart, I am still a small town girl. My soul is attached to my hometown and so it will be till my last breath. Though earlier I was so critical about life in a small town, today I realise that there are so many things about my home town that are missing in metro cities. In small towns, people are simple, reliable and down to earth. They are not materialistic. They do not leave anyone to die on the roads, in case of a mishap. Neighbours are always helpful and they don't ignore you or look through you when they meet you in any part of the world. They may not be glamorous like the people of big cities but yes, they are very clean hearted. Today, whenever I feel that I am lost in the crowd of a big city, I visit my home town to relax and regain my strength. I love to be there because it gives me peace.

In my father's friends' circle, many of the children got jobs in cities like Gurgaon and Bangalore. My father used to discuss these things at home. "You know my colleague's son is settled in Gurgaon. He's got a good job in some IT company. He will go to the US for his project work. He is very lucky."

Such news always inspired me. I started dreaming about my life. I wasn't sure if my parents would ever allow me to take up a job out of Yamuna Nagar, but I was bold and determined and promised to work hard day and night to make my career, earn a lot of money and fulfil my dreams.

A year later, I passed my second year of graduation and was promoted to the final year. The same year I went with my mother to meet my maternal grandmother in Lakhna. I remember I was in my teens and I was travelling with my mother in a reserved compartment. When the train stopped at Delhi I peeped out of the window to look at the Delhi crowd. Since my childhood, I had noticed the difference in the lifestyle between the big and the small cities. I was fascinated by the way of life in metro cities.

A few minutes later, when the train started to depart from the New Delhi railway station, a boy dressed in loose cargo pants, T shirt and floaters, with a small bag hanging from his shoulder, holding a rolled up newspaper in his hand rushed to our compartment. He had a reserved seat which happened to be opposite my seat. My mother was sleeping. The boy sat down. We both had a window seat. He glanced at me once and then started reading the newspaper. I was vacantly looking at the trees, railway tracks, electricity poles and green fields that were passing by in a blur. Suddenly I heard the boy say, "Could you please shift your bag a little bit so that I can keep my bag under your seat, there isn't any space anywhere else." I looked up at the boy and said, "Sure." I shifted my bag to the left to make some space. He kept his bag there and thanked me.

After sometime, the boy started chatting with me, "Where are you going?"

"I'm going to meet my maternal grandmother. Where are you going?" I asked.

"I am going to Kanpur to meet my parents. I live in Delhi and usually go on weekends to see my parents."

"Do you study in Delhi?" I asked out of curiosity.

"No, I am an MBA and I'm working in a company," he paused and asked me, "So where is your home town?"

"I live in Yamuna Nagar."

"Oh, Yamuna Nagar! I've visited that place two times. It is a small town – a little better than a village," he said with an impish smile.

That sentence irritated me a lot. I thought it was ridiculous. "What do you mean by it is no better than a village? It's a small city but it has all the facilities in terms of education and industry and people live a good life there. What's so special about Kanpur? I've visited that place once and I didn't like it at all. Anyway, you can't pass such comments about my city."

It's normal human nature that many times we don't appreciate what we have, yet when someone else criticises it, we don't like it.

The boy kept quiet for few minutes. He then smiled at me and said, "Please don't be angry. I don't want to hurt you."

When I regained my composure, I said, "It's alright. Tell me, which company do you work in?"

"First tell me, what's your name, pretty lady?" he said, trying to act smart.

I felt a little awkward as a complete stranger was calling me a pretty lady.

I insisted, "No, first you tell me your name."

He burst into peals of laughter and replied, "My name is Aakash Pandey."

"My name is Naina," I said and turned my face to the window.

"I work in a company that makes toys. I am the Assistant Manager there," he said, trying to impress me.

For the first time in my life I was meeting a mature and well settled boy who was not from Yamuna Nagar. Both of us enjoyed talking to each other.

Aakash asked me, "So what are you doing?"

"I am in B Sc. Computer Science, Final Year. I want to be a software engineer, so after graduation, I'll do my MCA."

"Do you know when there is recession, IT companies are the ones that are most affected and often people lose their jobs?"

"I'm not afraid of such things. I know that the trend in IT is like this only and these days people are losing their jobs due to recession. But I'm sure that after three years when I complete my MCA, I'll get a good job."

"Oh! I'm impressed by your confidence but don't be complacent. Do you know companies only visit reputed universities and colleges? They don't pick students from small private institutes. So never do your graduation or post-graduation from some private college."

I didn't know what to say so I just smiled in reply.

"Naina you have a lovely smile. But must you smile at everything I say?"

I stopped smiling immediately and started looking outside the window in anger. I didn't speak to him for the next few minutes. I wanted to hit him hard on his jaws but couldn't do anything.

He laughed again as he was enjoying the look on my face. He said, "Hey! Why are you getting angry? I was just kidding. Come on, talk to me. Let me tell you one thing - your smile is actually very beautiful."

I was fuming. I turned my face to him and asked him, "Are you a flirt?"

He laughed again. This time I could see his big teeth coated with a brown layer of tobacco, locally called gutka. "Well", I said to myself, "That's the sign of a typical UP boy."

He closed his mouth and spoke while swallowing the gutka in his mouth, "You look like a mature girl but actually I see you are just a kid. I didn't know that a girl could be so straight forward. I'm not a flirt. But I am pretty comfortable talking to girls as I have so many friends who are girls. We have such healthy conversations. It might appear strange to you as you're from a small town and obviously very narrow minded."

"You say there are so many girls in your group but tell me, do you like any one of them? I mean is there anyone who is special for you?" I tried to investigate.

"Yes, I had a girlfriend. She was very beautiful and tall just like you. You remind me of her."

I was shocked to hear this. "So what happened then? Did she leave you?"

"No, I left her as I knew that I'd never be able to marry her."

"You guys are so mean. Someone loved you and you refused to marry her. Then why did you even start the relationship?"

"Sweetheart, you need to be mature. It is not necessary that every love relationship should end in marriage. Love is altogether different from marriage. Many things may be acceptable in love but not in marriage. When you marry someone then you have to consider all aspects of your life with your partner-to-be. I couldn't marry her as she was very beautiful and I cannot afford to look after a beautiful wife. I belong to a backward society and I cannot protect her all the time. Some people might even be after her life and such a situation would disturb my life too."

"Boy, is this a silly reason to leave someone!"

I grimaced at his thoughts and took my eyes off him. I bent down to fasten the strap of my sandal. Aakash suddenly said, "Can I say something?"

"Yes?" I looked at him questioningly.

"You have horrible feet."

I quickly dragged my feet back and hid them under the seat. I was embarrassed as I knew that my feet were the worst part of my body.

I felt very conscious and looked away. It gave him ample time to stare at me from head to toe.

"But overall, you are very beautiful, your eyes are deep, and you have pretty pink lips," he reassured me.

My heart beat fast and my pulse started racing. I took a few minutes to catch my breath as so many bewildered thoughts rushed through my head. For the next few hours we didn't say anything but Aakash kept looking at me.

Many thoughts and feelings surged through me and I could not control my emotions. I said, "For the first time in my life I've talked so much to a stranger. I seem to have no control over the feelings that are rushing through me."

"What are you feeling ma'am?"

"I don't know but it's something that I can't express."

Aakash asked me, "Do you have an email id? I'll write to you."

I didn't want any kind of friendship between us so I replied calmly, "No, I don't have an email id."

Aakash fumbled in his pockets and took out his business card. He stretched his hand towards me.

I too, stretched my hand out to him but suddenly stopped in the middle. I gave him a questioning look, fighting the thought uppermost in my mind whether I should take it or not.

Suddenly, he kept his card on my palm. "This is my visiting card. Come and meet me if you get a chance to visit Delhi in future. You can also call me if you want to talk to me." His company's name, address, cell number and his designation were written on the card.

I threw it into the side pocket of my bag imagining that I would forget about it if I let it lie buried under all my belongings. That way I'd never call him. Sometimes, we try to fool ourselves but we all know that doesn't always work, does it?

We were about to arrive in Etawah in a few minutes. I woke my mother up and collected our luggage. My mother walked up to door but I was still at my seat. Aakash shook my hand and said goodbye. I could feel the warmth in his handshake and it sent a tingling sensation through my veins.

My mother and I got down at the station. Aakash was looking at me from the window. I gave him a smile. When the train left the station, I felt bad. Suddenly I felt that I was leaving something behind and some change was taking place within me. I felt I had lost my heart. I wanted to go back to the train and talk for some time more with him.

> At that time, I did not know that that guy was a big flirt. It wasn't my fault. It was the immaturity of my teenage years. I was falling in love with a boy who was smart, mature and knew how to flatter a girl.

My mother and I reached my grandmother's house. One day had passed but I was still thinking about Aakash. I was lost in some other world. I missed him. Two days later, I took out Aakash's visiting card form my bag and called him from a telephone booth. My hands were trembling as I dialled his number. The phone rang and Aakash picked up the receiver and said, "Hello."

I kept quiet.

I heard him say "Hello" once again from the other side and said, "Hello."

"Who's this?"

"Hi, I am Naina."

"Hey Naina, how are you?"

"I am fine, thanks."

"So ma'am, finally, you called me. What's up?"

"I am at my grandmother's place."

"Do they know that you are talking to me?"

"No, they don't know."

"Cool. So what made you call me?"

"Nothing, I just felt like talking to you, so I called up. Something has happened to me. This time I am not enjoying my visit to my grandmother's place. I am just lost somewhere."

"Ma'am let me also know where you're lost."

"I don't know. Anyway I'll disconnect as I have to go back home. Everyone must be wondering where I am."

"Ok. You can call me any time. Bye."

I came back to my grandmother's place. No one came to know where I had gone. I was so happy after talking to him. I kept thinking about him all the time. I started calling him up twice a week.

One month passed and it was time to go back to Yamuna Nagar. My mother and I were on the train going back to Yamuna Nagar. The train stopped at Delhi station. I looked out of the window. My eyes searched every corner of the station. My mother asked me, "What's wrong? What are you looking for?"

My face suddenly turned pale. I paused and said, "Nothing. I am just checking to see if we can buy some tea from a tea stall at the station." After a few seconds, a tea vendor came inside the compartment. He called out in Hindi, "Chai le lo, chai le lo, do ruppai mein," – offering us tea at two rupees per cup. Mother gave him four rupees and asked for two cups of tea. The train left the station and I wondered, "God, will we ever meet again?"

I sat at the window seat. There was an unusual silence in the compartment. I looked at the passing trees, electric poles, fields, railway tracks and children trying to race against the train. My mind was blank. I did not even realise that the train had reached Ambala station. We rushed to the bus stand near the station to catch a bus to Yamuna Nagar. It was already evening by the time we reached home.Dad and Priyanshu were waiting for us.

This time Priyanshu hadn't gone to grandmother's place with us as he was preparing for the engineering common entrance test. He appeared for the exams and passed the entrance tests of Kurukshetra University and Punjab University. All of us were very happy and excited. My father received a letter to attend the counselling session and reserve a seat in one of the reputed colleges.

In spite of the happiness all of us felt at my brother's success, my father was worried because he wasn't sure how much money he would have to shell out per year for Priyanshu's fees. Next day he left in the morning with my uncle Nagendra and Priyanshu to attend the counselling session. They came back in the evening. I opened the door excitedly and asked Priyanshu, "Hey, where have you got your seat?"

Priyanshu entered home with a glum face. He looked crestfallen and there was no smile on his face. He spoke with a heavy heart, "I will never get a seat because of our dear Dad."

I asked Uncle, "What happened? Why is he so upset?"

Uncle replied, "Your father has a very small heart. Priyanshu was offered seats in two colleges and we were asked to pay ten thousand rupees to reserve one seat. I asked your father to sign and reserve the seat. But he got frightened. His face turned pale and his hands started shaking while he held the pen to sign the register to book a seat. Suddenly, he left the documents and came back. I asked him what he was thinking of and that we would surely lose the seat if we didn't pay up right away. Your father said that he couldn't afford the fees of forty thousand rupees per year. Priyanshu would be completing his B. Tech in four years and Naina would also be studying at the same time. How would he afford such big expenses? He was afraid that if he wasn't able to pay the fees at any time then Priyanshu would have to leave his studies."

I sat down and held my head in my hands. It seemed to me that everyone was in mourning. In life, as I had known it, whenever we had lost hope, it was always my father who would fix everything for us and give us courage. Today it was my father who felt hopeless and no one knew what to do.

I regained my strength and took up the challenge of breaking this impasse. "I want to thank God that I was not able to clear the engineering entrance exams. If I had cleared my entrance exams I'd have suffered more and that pain would have been more than the pain of failure. Because my father cannot afford to educate us further. You are not a courageous man, Dad. You have a small heart like that of a sparrow. You are a man who can only dream but can't fulfil them. You know what, you'll always be a middle class man who rides a bicycle even on cold nights to travel miles to teach rich men's kids so that he can earn some money for the higher education of his own children. He will never eat in expensive restaurants so that he can save money for his kids. Now when the time has come to show the world that you struggled hard in life to give an edge to your son's career, you are hiding your face because you think you cannot afford our education. Then why did you make your whole life so wretched by struggling all the time? Why can't you afford to educate your son? You can do everything. You just need to be brave, Dad. You will have to try, we cannot lose this chance. Priyanshu has got an opportunity to make his life and if you don't book a seat for him, he will spend his whole life like you. Take out your savings and we will pay his fees. This is the day you were waiting for. Be brave Dad."

> The situation seemed surreal to me like a Hindi film scene when the heroine goes to a temple on a stormy night and gives an impassioned speech to the deity there about the injustices in her life. Just after she opens her heart, a flower falls from the statue indicating that God has been moved by the lady's words and with his divine blessings everything in her life would change for the better.

After this long lecture, my father sat down and thought for a moment. He then said, "Ok, I will go tomorrow to book a seat in an engineering college for my son. Thank you Naina, you've opened my eyes."

I know I was being harsh to my father. I should never have spoken like this to him. But it worked. He went the next day and booked a seat for Priyanshu in one of the reputed colleges in Punjab. This incident increased my confidence and I felt victorious.

While Priyanshu was all set to join his new college (for the first time in his life he was going to live in a hostel), I passed my final year of graduation and I knew what to do next. I wanted to do my Masters in Computer Application.

I confided in my father, "Please Dad, send me out of Yamuna Nagar for coaching classes just as you had sent Priyanshu to Chandigarh to prepare for his engineering entrance examinations. I will also prepare for MCA entrance examinations and get admission in a good university after passing the exam. I cannot get good coaching here."

My father was wild. He acted like a commander getting tough with his troops. His big eyes popped out like those of a rabbit's, he raised his index finger and shook it sternly, "No, I won't send you anywhere. You're a girl and we can't leave you alone in any city."

I revolted, "Dad. If you don't want to send me anywhere then it's fine but I promise you that I'll work hard and clear these exams without any coaching. The day will come when you'll have to send me out of this place."

I took up this challenge and studied hard for the exams. I appeared for the entrance exams of Shimla, Punjab and Kurukshetra Universities. I cleared two of them. Now it was time for me to choose a college. My family ordered me not to choose any college out of Yamuna Nagar. According to them, I'd be more comfortable in a college that was near home and this way I could stay with my family. In the end, I had to choose a college in Yamuna Nagar itself.

After a few days, I joined the college. It was like a small institute with hardly seven to eight rooms, a washroom, an assembly area and a small parking space. I had always dreamt of studying on a big campus so this seemed like a disaster. Still I didn't lose hope. I kept my expectations high and made up my mind to learn as much as I could from this small institute. There were many rules in the college that seemed to lack logic but the students were clever enough to find ways of breaking the rules. The first day of college was full of fun. There were thirty students in MCA first year. When the final year students saw the freshers, they got excited as they would have a good time ragging their juniors. On the first day when I entered my classroom, I saw that all the girls were sitting on one side while the boys were sitting on the other side. It seemed as if they were going to play an INDIA - PAKISTAN match. Most of the girls were from Yamuna Nagar. Only a few belonged to other cities. I also found some of my old college friends and this made me feel comfortable. After some time, a teacher entered the class. He was smart and intelligent. He introduced himself and asked everyone to introduce themselves.

One boy stood up and said confidently in English, "Myself Mohan, and I come from Karnal. I am doing my graduation from Guru Harkishan Public College." He had obviously learnt English in a small school in a small town.

Another boy stood up and tried to copy his friend, "Hi, I am Dinu. I am coming from Hoshiarpur city. I like surfing, reading etc."

Hardly two or three people could introduce themselves using correct English while most spoke incorrect English in their Haryana, UP or Punjabi accents. My friends and I laughed at the dismal English spoken by our classmates. I thought to myself, "These days, anyone can get admission easily, irrespective of the required skills or qualifications as there are so many private institutes. These institutes are more of commercial establishments rather than educational institutes."

After listening to all the introductions the teacher said, "I welcome all of you and hope all of you will get good jobs in big IT companies after college. I hope that each one of you has good technical knowledge as all of you are computer graduates. But for you the most important thing to learn is communication skills. You should improve your communication skills. Remember, companies demand this skill while hiring people."

After the first lecture, a few more teachers came in and similar introduction sessions continued in every class. Every teacher had his own style. They were flaunting the fact that their institute was very good and many of their students had been placed in the top five Indian IT companies. The truth was that no company had ever come there for any campus interview. All students who had been placed in any of the big companies had done their own hard work to get jobs. They had spent months searching for jobs after passing out.

In the evening, the final year students came into the class. They asked all the juniors to go and stand in the front of the classroom facing the benches. The seniors, most of who looked like miscreants, went and sat on the back benches. One of them asked the juniors to introduce themselves and also described the way in which they were to do so.

"Each one of you will wish us bending at an angle of ninety degrees. This means, that you have to bend the upper half of your body towards the earth at an angle of ninety degrees and introduce yourself in pure Hindi. We will punish those who commit mistakes."

Then all the seniors looked at the new faces carefully and asked those who were smiling to come forward. Two boys and two girls came forward. I was one of them. They asked me to introduce myself to them. I told them in Hindi that my name was Naina. I had graduated from Gayatri Girls College and that I had scored 77 percent marks. My hobbies were singing, dancing and cooking.

One of the seniors said, "Oh madam, if your hobby is singing then sing a song for all of us. Better still; call one of your friends to dance while you sing."

I randomly picked on my friend Dinesh to dance while I sang. He stared at me and whispered in my ears, "Hey, why did you call my name, I don't even know how to dance."

I started singing a Hindi film song while Dinesh stood facing me.

"Jo haal dil ka idhar ho raha hai, wo haal dil ka udhar ho raha hai."

Dinesh started dancing like one who was drunk. He looked so funny that I started laughing.

All the seniors said, "Hey, you can't laugh. Only we have the right to laugh. Dinesh you should stand facing your back to Naina so that she may not laugh." This entertainment went on for half an hour until the last bell rang for the day. Everyone left in a happy mood.

For one and a half months, such episodes went on between the seniors and the juniors. Some senior boys fell in love with the junior girls and others became good friends. I became very popular among the seniors because of my singing talent, confidence and presentation skills.

After two months, there was a fresher's party in our college and I won the title of Miss Fresher. Along with my studies, I continued sending emails to Aakash. My brother smelt something fishy. He cracked the password of my email id, checked my emails and actually went and told my parents everything. My father asked me the reason, "Why do you talk to that guy?" I had no answer. He warned me, "You should concentrate on your studies rather than doing anything like this. If you don't listen to me, I will stop your studies in the middle and you will get married very soon." I was scared but I didn't stop talking to Aakash. Instead, I started calling him from a public telephone booth outside my institute.

Gradually, Aakash started showing his true nature. He was a real flirt. I tried controlling my feelings for him but I couldn't resist my attraction towards him. As time passed, Aakash started discouraging me. He always told me, "You're a girl from a small town and you don't know anything about life in big cities. You're very narrow minded. You don't like what I say. You aren't mature and you certainly aren't as stylish as Delhi girls are."

I was fed up with all this. One day, I was trying to divert my mind from Aakash to my studies. All the things that Aakash had said were going around in my mind. I was feeling very low and lonely. I started crying. My mother noticed this and asked me, "What's happened? Why are you crying like this?" This made me cry bitterly.

I opened my heart to my mother, "Mom, I want to become part of a big city. I want to earn everything that I can for myself in this lifetime. I want to do all the things that Dad could not do because of his responsibilities. I want to show this world who I am and what I am capable of. I want to make Dad and you proud of me. I know, one day, I will become an inspiration for all the other girls in our family. Many people underestimate me."

My mother listened to all this and said, "What's happened to you? Did someone say something to you? I don't know about your future but I will tell you only one thing. I know you're hardworking. One day this hard work will pay and you will get what you want from life. Don't lose heart."

From that day onwards, I never spoke to Aakash and decided to just follow my dream. After I completed the first year of college, my classmates decided to enroll for extra computer courses that would help them get jobs in good IT companies. They decided to go to Delhi for two months and join the advanced Java course in a reputed computer institute. I also wanted to join them but I wasn't sure if my parents would send me to Delhi. I thought of an idea. One of my aunts, Leela, was staying in Delhi with her family. I called her up and told her that I needed her help. I told her that I wanted to come to Delhi to do a computer course and asked if I could stay at her place for two months as my father wouldn't allow me to stay as a paying guest elsewhere. Leela Aunty was happy about the idea and agreed readily without any hesitation. I was grateful for her support.

Then I told my father about my plans, "Dad, a few of my classmates are going to Delhi to join the advanced Java course. I also want to go with them. It will help me to get a job. I have spoken to Leela Aunty and she has agreed to let me stay at her place."

My father thought for a moment and said, "Ok, I'm happy that you're going to stay at your aunt's place. This way you will be under her supervision. Do you know which computer institute you will join? Have you enquired about it?"

I said, "Yes, my classmates have found out about it and we'll be joining the same institute."

A few days later, I packed my bags and left for Delhi with Dad. I was very excited as for two months I'd be out of Yamuna Nagar and would enjoy the life of a big city. We reached my aunt's place. Leela Aunty lived in a two roomed flat in South Delhi at R.K. Puram. It was a nice place with a lot of parks and markets around. Though the flat was small, Leela Aunty made place for me and my luggage in one room. Dad left for Yamuna Nagar the following day.

I used my uncle's cell phone and called my classmates who had already arrived in Delhi one week before. I called Jassi, "Hey Fatty, how are you? So have you decided which institute we are going to join?"

"Naina, here the institutes are charging twelve to fourteen thousand rupees for Java - computer language course and you know, so far, we haven't even been able to find a suitable place to stay in, in South Extension. It has been one week and we've already spent ten thousand rupees on our food and other expenses. It is hard to survive in Delhi. You're lucky that you're staying at your relative's place and aren't facing issues like food and accommodation."

"I'm a girl and my parents would never allow me to stay as a paying guest in a place like Delhi. So I'm staying here. My aunt is good to me. She has supported me. By the way, what are we going to do now? I told my father that you guys have already chosen an institute and only on this basis did he allow me to come here. I want to meet all of you."

"Ok. Come to South Ex. tomorrow at 10:30 A.M. We will meet you in front of JNIIT."

It was the first time that I was visiting Delhi. I did not know anything about the various localities nor was I aware of modes of transport in Delhi but I had no choice but to handle all this by myself.

I asked Leela Aunty's husband, "Uncle, I want to go to South Ex. tomorrow. Could you please tell me how to reach there?"

He said, "In Delhi, there is no problem about commuting. Here, the government has provided us with several facilities like buses, taxis and auto rickshaws. You will get at least ten buses for a single route but you should be careful while travelling. The first thing that you should be careful about is your wallet and cell phone. In a crowded bus, money and cell phones are stolen from the pockets of passengers and they come to know about it only when they fumble in their pockets while paying for bus tickets. There are many buses that go from R.K. Puram to South Extension. You can get route numbers 865, 864 and 727 from the main road itself. I also go to office by bus. Tomorrow I will show you the way and next time onwards you can go by yourself."

I was grateful, "Thanks a lot. So I'll go with you tomorrow. One more thing, Uncle, Dad bought me a second hand mobile because I was coming to Delhi. It'll be easy for me to contact someone especially if I need something. Could you please buy me a sim card from a market nearby?"

My uncle and I went out in the evening and bought a prepaid sim card from a mobile shop in the local market of Sector-7 in R.K. Puram.

"It will be activated in one hour. Then you can call up your friends and parents and give them your number. Ok, so you're all set now for your stay in Delhi. Are you feeling hungry?"

Even though I wasn't hungry, Uncle wanted me to try something new. "I'd like to buy roasted chicken for you from a famous shop here. Your aunt and I love the chicken they make. Now that you're in Delhi for two months, I'd like you to taste the delicious food here."

Next morning I got ready. I dressed up in salwar kameez. My aunt gave us packed lunch before we left for our respective destinations. Uncle and I stood at a small bus stand on the main road. I carefully read the information board (it had the bus number and the destination) of every passing bus. Suddenly bus number 864 came and stopped at the bus stand. It was a little crowded. My uncle and I got into the bus from the rear. I saw my uncle was moving towards the front of the bus where people were buying tickets from the conductor.

Uncle told the conductor, "Two for South Ex."

The conductor asked him to pay ten rupees and gave him two tickets. My uncle explained the route to me, "Naina, this bus takes hardly ten to fifteen minutes to cover the distance from R.K. Puram to South Ex. The first stop will be Mohan Singh Market, then Sarojini Nagar, then Safdarjang Hospital, then AIIMS and then South Ex."

After fifteen minutes, the bus stopped at South Extension. Both of us got off at the bus stop. He showed me JNIIT which was on the other side of road. "Ok, you can go and meet your friends now; I'll leave for my office. Bye, I'll see you in the evening. You can get the same bus while going back," Uncle waved to me and left.

I was surprised to see Delhi, its crowds and its big showrooms. All the people were well dressed. Everyone had their own style statement. I didn't see a single girl without lip liner, lip shade, fashionable clothes, big earrings, footwear, sun shades and colourful and stylish handbags. One couldn't judge if a girl actually belonged to a middle class family or a high class family. Here girls dressed up every day as if they were going to celebrate Diwali. Well, I guess that's fun and it imparts a feel good factor to everyone, as the saying goes – "When you wear something good, you feel good". If that is true, then I guess the people of Delhi always feel good. Boys, however, were seen wearing long kurtas with jeans, listening to music, wearing chappals. I found that I was very simple as compared to the other girls. In fact, I reminded myself, at home I wasn't even allowed to wear jeans.

I reached JNIIT and met my friends. The institute had a big, conspicuous building. I could see many people going in and coming out. Girls with open hair, long earrings, big bags, short dresses, with notebooks in their hands could be seen sitting and chatting on the lawn. This was my first exposure of how students enjoy their lives in metro cities. All small town girls are awed by such girls and the glamour of big cities and I was one of them. I wanted to look like them. Those of us who belong to small towns have only seen actresses on the screen wearing such clothes ;in real life, we've never ever seen or worn anything like that.

My friends were distraught, "We don't know which institute to choose. Let's go together to all the computer institutes in South Ex."

We sweated profusely as we roamed the streets of South Extension visiting all the institutes one after another on that hot sunny day of June. After a while we felt hungry and thirsty. One of my friends said, "Let's go to some stall to eat lunch."

"I've got my lunch. We'll share it," I showed them the big lunch box that my aunt had packed for me.

We went to a road side stall where they were selling yellow curry and rice for twenty five rupees. Each one of us bought a plate of this rice and curry and we ate it along with my lunch. It was almost three in the afternoon. We decided to relax. We roamed around in South Extension and visited the big showrooms there. My friends openly stared at the Delhi girls and started talking about them in whispers.

"Stop it guys, behave like gentlemen. Don't stare at girls so obviously and stop talking nonsense," I said, while kicking one of my friends in an effort to stop him from misbehaving.

"Hey, Delhi girls are so attractive that it's difficult to resist them."

I looked around and was shocked to see a group of girls wearing tight fitting tops that highlighted their figures and short pants that exposed their beautiful long, smooth and fair legs. They had long, open hair and wore makeup. As if this was not enough, some of these attractive looking girls were also smoking in great style. They talked in English interspersed with bits of Hindi. I immediately felt the difference in their urban way of speaking and the almost rustic way in which we would talk to our friends in Yamuna Nagar. I was disturbed to see all this, as in real life I had never seen girls wearing such short clothes, let alone girls smoking and that too in public places.

I wasn't able to digest this at all. If any girl in Yamuna Nagar had done it, then the next day, she would have become the talk of the town and everybody would have discriminated against her for straying from the straight and narrow path.

I looked at my wrist watch and saw that it was five o'clock. I said good bye to my friends. We decided to meet at the same place the following day and choose the institute that would be the best for all of us.

I caught bus number 727 to go back home. On the first day itself I felt confident as now, I could catch a bus all by myself. My uncle arrived after half an hour of my reaching home. Aunty made tea for all of us and we sat and chatted over tea. I told them what a crowded and lively place I had found South Extension to be. I spoke about the big showrooms and the stylish Delhi girls. And how shocked I was to see them smoking!

"Welcome to Delhi, my dear! It is totally different from Yamuna Nagar. Here you will see girls are more modern and broad minded. They wear what they like and do what they want. It doesn't matter to them if it actually suits our Indian culture or not," Leela Aunty said all this with a smile on her face.

"I've seen very few girls wearing salwar kameez. Most of the girls are dressed in jeans, stylish tops, skirts and shorts while I couldn't wear jeans even at home," I said, frowning all the while.

"Don't worry. Every Sunday we have a Sunday market in sector 7. We'll go there and you can buy jeans, stylish tops and funky earrings at reasonable rates. The shopkeeper first asks for a high price but after bargaining, he gives it at a cheaper rate," Aunty tried to make me happy.

"Ok, that sounds great!" I said excitedly.

In the next few days, my friends and I scouted around and decided on which computer institute to join. We asked the institute owner to provide us training at discounted rates. Each one of us paid ten thousand rupees for a two month course.

Now every morning I caught a bus and reached my institute. After class I spent time with a new girl who had joined the class. She became my new friend. We went to Planet M to listen to music, McDonald's for burgers and fries, browsed through book shops and enjoyed daal and rice at small stalls.

I started enjoying this phase of my life very much. On Sunday I went to the Sunday market with my aunt who was crazy about clothes and jewellery. Every Sunday she used to buy something. This was a temporary bazaar set up every Sunday, something along the lines of a flea market found in other parts of the world. Though each vendor had to set up his shop in the open and within a small area, he made sure that his shop looked attractive enough to catch the attention of customers. The shiny stuff looked even shinier under the big lights. Shops were set up in rows which faced each other and people in and around that area rushed to buy things at cheap rates. When I entered the market, the one thing that attracted me the most were the bangle and jewellery shops. No market in India is complete without these shops. They always attract ladies, who in any case, are the best customers anywhere in the world. I bought some clothes and bangles for just two hundred and fifty rupees.

One vendor was shouting, "Hey come on and buy two tops for twenty rupees." Leela Aunty and I ran to that stall which had a huge pile of tops. We spent twenty minutes in an attempt to find some tops in the latest designs. I could see how much time girls spend in order to appear attractive. Everyone was trying to look for something special in that pile. Finally, I bought two tops for twenty rupees.

Now it was time for me to buy a pair of jeans. My aunt took me to another stall where the shopkeeper was selling a pair of jeans for one hundred rupees only. We picked one and started bargaining. My aunt told the shopkeeper, "Give us some discount. Sell it to us for sixty five rupees only." The shopkeeper refused saying that his price was fixed. My aunt threw the pair back and started walking away from his stall. I followed my aunt and asked her why he would give it for sixty five rupees. "Let's buy it for hundred rupees," I suggested, afraid that I would have to go back disappointed.

My aunt said, "Don't worry. Keep walking, he will call us back."

And sure enough, much to my surprise, he did! "Ok Aunty, come back. I can give it to you for seventy five rupees but not less than that. What will be my profit otherwise?"

My aunt gave me a wicked smile and accepted his offer. Thus, we got a pair of jeans for seventy five rupees only.

I was elated, "Wow Aunty, that sure was a good deal. So I've bought all the stuff for only ninety five rupees. But I shouldn't spend more as Dad will have to bear these unnecessary expenses."

Aunty was impatient, "Oh please don't think so much. Tell me, do you have shoes to wear with your jeans?"

"No, but I've seen girls wearing high heel shoes with jeans. They must be expensive."

"In this market you can get good shoes at cheap rates. Come, we'll buy a pair for you. Don't worry, I'll pay for it", she offered.

We went to a vendor. He had arranged all the shoe sizes on a white sheet on the road. I could see big brand names embossed on the displayed pairs of shoes. So this was the selling strategy of these small vendors, I realised, to use big brand names to sell their cheap stuff which lasted only for a few months.

I chose a pair of light brown high heeled shoes and asked the vendor how much he would charge. He offered me the pair for one hundred and fifty rupees, tempting me with the line that I wouldn't be able to pick up such a pair anywhere else. My aunt asked him to sell it for a hundred rupees. Once again, I marvelled at my aunt's negotiating skills when the vendor readily agreed.

I took the shoes and felt content. We also ate the popular north Indian snack of chana bhatura at a stall. Though there were flies buzzing around, it didn't bother either the seller or the customer. In India, we are quite used to flies while eating at road side stalls. It's almost as if it adds to the taste of the food.

While enjoying a bite of the bhatura, I told Aunty that I wouldn't buy anything else that month, considering my small budget but in the following month, I would buy some earrings.

Aunty was sporting about the whole thing, "Sure and enjoy your stay in Delhi. You are beautiful and you should be stylish too." Within two months, I changed my appearance.

Meanwhile, my aunt's neighbours also got to know me. My aunt was an enterprising lady and had started a beauty parlour at home. During the weekend, ladies of every age group visited her parlour. It didn't matter how old a lady was, each and everyone wanted a beautiful glowing skin and clean arms and legs. One customer would mean one full hour of entertainment, including gossip about all the neighbours.

My aunt knew selling tactics. Not only would she gossip nonstop with her customers, she would also suggest extra beauty treatments to them. I remember one incident. One day, a lady came to the parlour for a facial. When Aunty asked her what kind of facial she wanted, the lady asked for the rate list. Aunty proudly displayed her rate chart:

Fruit facial – Rs. 250.00
Silver facial – Rs. 300.00
Gold facial – Rs. 700.00
Pearl facial – Rs. 550.00
Special glow facial - Rs. 800.00

The customer settled for a fruit facial. My aunt swung into action trying to convince the customer, "Oh come on! A fruit facial lasts for one week only. You have a fair complexion. You will look more beautiful after a special glow facial. I'll apply bleach before the facial just for seventy rupees and you'll be happy to see the glow on your face. You will definitely thank me after the facial.

"Ok, but it seems a bit expensive."

"No, no, it's not all that expensive. I'm giving you a discounted price compared to other parlours. If you get the same facial done from some other parlour, they'll charge you at least thousand rupees."

"Ok ji, then I'll go in for it." Finally the customer was convinced and Aunty was happy as the customer was ready to pay more.

By the time the facial started, the customer and my aunt were chatting like childhood friends. I used to enjoy such funny moments.

My days passed cheerfully. I worked hard at my computer course and I grasped it very well. Along with my studies, I enjoyed shopping at cheap rates in the Sunday market, listening to music at Planet M, Radio FM in local buses, going out for coffee and burgers with my friends in South Extension, watching movies with my aunt and uncle at Sangam cinema and visiting Malai Mandir on Saturdays. I loved the time I spent in Delhi.

Many times it so happens that when you are happy in life, something takes place that suddenly kills your happiness. After some days, I got some messages on my cell phone from an unknown number. One day, when I was having piping hot tea and enjoying the rain standing in the balcony of Aunty's sweet little flat in R.K. Puram, a message flashed on my cell phone. I couldn't identify the number but out of curiosity, I read the message. "Hi Naina. I love you a lot. I could never tell you this when we were together. I miss you a lot. I want to meet you. Guess who I am?" I was flabbergasted seeing this weird message. I could not, for the life of me, understand who would send me such a message and how could anyone get hold of my Delhi number. I typed "Shut up" and sent it to the same number. Again my cell phone beeped and again there was another message from the same number, "Dear, don't be so rude. Why do you always ignore me? You are my sweetheart. By the way, why can't you guess my name?"

I lost my temper and called that number but no one picked up. I sent a harsh reply on the same number. Within a minute I got a reply. "Sweetheart, I'm the same person who sang a song for you once when we were in the twelfth standard. It has been four years and I still love you. Will you marry me?"

I was shocked to see that the message was from the boy who liked me when I was studying in the school where my uncle used to teach. At that time he couldn't utter a single word to me as he was scared of my uncle but now he was sending me stupid messages. I didn't want to hear from that guy again so I thought for a moment and replied, "Don't try to act smart. If you send me one more message, I'll call the police and my fiancé. They'll teach you the real meaning of love and marriage."

After that I didn't get any message from him as I had told him indirectly that I was engaged and there was no point in following a girl who had already committed herself to someone. I had learnt from my friends that this was the best way to get rid of such Romeos - such statements were sure to dampen their spirit.

My two months in Delhi were over and now, it was time to go back home.

I packed my belongings and left for Yamuna Nagar. I felt upset upon reaching my hometown as I was back to a life which was so different from life in a metro. I was missing Delhi. One of the good things that had come out of it, apart from my studies, was that I had become a little stylish.

After the vacations, it was time to go back to college. In the morning, I got ready to go to college. My mother was in the kitchen and my father had gone out for a morning walk. "Naina come and have your breakfast and take your packed lunch for college also," my mother screamed from the kitchen. I could hear her clearly in the bedroom.

I quickly went to the kitchen and gulped my breakfast. I wore jeans and a T shirt and started my scooty (my father had given me his scooty when he bought the scooter). While I was on my way, my father noticed me but I drove away at a high speed to escape from his sight. When I reached college, my friends paid me a big compliment, "Hey, you look stunning!"

The teacher asked everyone what they had learnt in the vacations. We proudly told him that we had completed the advanced Java course in Delhi. The teacher was quite happy to see our progress. He said that there would be many job opportunities for those who knew Java. So all we had to do was to keep on updating ourselves on advanced technologies.

After college when I reached home, my mother saw me in jeans. She asked me, "Why did you wear jeans? You know very well that you aren't allowed to wear such clothes in this house. If any of your uncles or your father sees you like this, they will feel very upset and scold you very badly."

I said, "Mom, there is no need to listen to everyone all the time. Mark my words Mom, when my uncles have daughters my age, they will never say no to their kids for anything. All my cousins will wear jeans and T shirts. I don't know why you have to decide your life and your children's lifestyle according to what they say. Do we have our own life or not? I am mature. I have a healthy college life. There is no harm in wearing such clothes and I want to wear it. You can tell Dad what I have told you. From now on, I will do what I like and I won't listen to anyone."

From that day onwards, I started wearing jeans. I was enjoying my college life. I worked hard and scored good percent in every semester of MCA. I was getting more ambitious day by day.

I enjoyed my college life to the fullest. Very often, I gave rides to my friends on my scooty. But people always made fun of my scooty as it was very noisy - especially the humming sound it made when I started it. One day, while I was coming back home from college, I saw one of my seniors at the bus stop and I stopped my scooty to say "Hi" to him.

He teased me, "Ma'am my auto rickshaw is faster than your scooty. See, I've reached home and you've just covered one fourth of the distance you have to go. Leave this old scooty now."

I smiled and spoke confidently to him, "Don't worry, Sir. One day I'll have my own car and I'll be driving on the same roads where you are standing now. Mark my words. It's just a matter of time."

My senior looked at me in surprise and I left.

∞

I was in the second year of my post-graduation while my brother was doing his B.Tech at the same time. Every Saturday he used to come home and would go back to the hostel on Sunday night. Ever since he had started living in the hostel, his habits had changed. Whenever he came home, he would take charge of the television remote control and watch all English channels till three in the morning. The following day he would get up at twelve in the afternoon. Everyone was shocked to see the changes in him.

I asked him, "Hey, why you have changed so much? You don't sleep on time, you don't eat on time and you don't even get up on time. Also, I've never seen you studying hard. What's up dude? You're doing Mechanical Engineering, how come you're not serious about your studies? You know very well that our father has to do part time tuitions till ten in the night to save forty thousand rupees for one year."

"My dear sister, you know, even if I study just one night before my exam, I'll clear five out of seven exams in a semester, while my friends will fail in all the seven exams. Sometimes, my friends have to re-appear in all the fourteen exams of two semesters while this is not the case with me."

"Priyanshu, I know by God's grace you're brilliant, but what you lack is hard work. Even if you work just a little hard, your performance will be sky-high."

"Oh go on, I've seen your hard work. You are glued to books all the time but I can't be like you. Now just leave me alone, don't trouble me anymore. Let me watch an action movie. Go and bring some stuffed paranthas for me otherwise, I'll beat you."

"Shut up and go to hell. It is no use talking to you. I certainly won't bring anything for you to eat."

Priyanshu threw a pillow at my face and asked me to leave the room.

After one more year I started the final year of my post-graduation. Every student was worried about getting a job. We were waiting for campus selection. It was time for our institute to show their students that it was really worthwhile doing MCA from that institute and that they could get students placed in good IT companies.

By chance, a few of our senior students had been placed in one of the companies in Chandigarh at salaries of twenty thousand rupees per month. The institute loved to boast about this in front of the new students. When we were about to complete the fifth semester, the placement manager asked each one of us to submit a well drafted resume to him so that he could talk to a few of the companies and invite them to our institute for campus selection. The students always made fun of the placement manager, "Look at his communication skills. He speaks broken English and that too, with a regional accent. How can our teachers imagine that such a guy can represent our institute to renowned IT companies? Top IT companies don't have time to interact with such useless fellows. Also, he doesn't have any contacts in big companies. Now we realise that joining a four roomed private institute can't take us places. They are just small shops opened in small towns to make money from students. We'll have to use our own contacts to be placed in some company."

Students were required to complete a six month training programme with an IT company after their fifth semester and on the basis of the training completion certificates, they would get marks for the sixth semester. In the fifth semester, the placement manager called up two to three companies. Two of them were from the BPO sector and one was a small IT company in Chandigarh that hardly had fifteen employees. To us it seemed that if everyone had to work only in small IT companies then what was the need to spend lakhs of rupees to get a professional degree?

After seeing no hopes of placement from the institute, every student started doing their own homework. They used their contacts to get training in big IT companies. A few of them were successful as some of their relatives were able to arrange training in their companies but every- one was not that lucky.

> In small cities, people are not able to guide their children properly about their careers. They tend to get influenced by other people's children. If other people's sons or daughters become engineers or doctors, they feel that their child should also follow the same career path. They ask their children to join small local private institutes which have no value or reputation. This results in jobless degree holders. I know many students who passed out from small institutes two years back but are unemployed till date.

I had no contacts. In fact, I was the first one in my family to join the IT sector. I talked to my father about it. "Dad, do you have any contacts in Yamuna Nagar who could arrange my training in some IT company? You have taught many rich people's children in this town. All of them are industrialists. I'm sure they will have contacts in Delhi, Noida or Gurgaon. It would really help me."

My father said, "I don't know if anyone will entertain me. It is our need and not anyone else's. I will try, though I can't promise anything."

For one month my father tried to get in touch with all his contacts. He used to repeat the same lines over the phone, "Hello mister so and so, how are you? How is your son? I hope he's joined your business now. Actually I have called you for a reason. My daughter is doing her MCA from a local institute. As part of her curriculum, she needs to complete her training from an IT company. If you have any contacts, then please help us."

The person from the other side would answer, "Ok. I'll see if I can do something about it. I'll let you know'.

One month passed and nothing happened. One day I lashed out in frustration at my parents, "This is happening because of us. My career has been ruined. I had to join some stupid local institute and today no company knows that there is one poor Naina who secured above 75 percent marks throughout the course. She has the capability of working in a good company. I could easily have joined some better college outside Yamuna Nagar and how does it matter to anyone if I spent three years in a hostel. At least I would have been placed somewhere by now. But no, a girl should stay at home; otherwise, she might run away with a guy if she lives away from home."

My father said, "Don't shout at us. What we did was only for your good. You stayed with your family and enjoyed home food. You should ask the children who live in hostels. They miss the fact that they are away from home. You're saying all this because you have never been in such a situation."

I said, "What you're telling me is not true. I'm a girl, so you never wanted to send me away from home."

My father said, "Ok. Whatever has happened is over now. It's time to think about your training. We can visit the small IT companies in Chandigarh and request for your training. Chandigarh is near Yamuna Nagar and you can travel by bus every day. This way you will not have to stay outside your home town. Contact your friends and create a list of all the companies we can visit."

> As simple as that! My father is so innocent. He is very good at heart. He always wanted to do what was best for me but he belonged to such a society that taught him to believe that it was a sin to go beyond his conservative way of thinking. But today, I appreciate the fact that with time, he was able to change his way of thinking.

I made a list of all the companies and prepared my resume. There were small IT companies in Mohali near Chandigarh.

I decided I would visit all the companies with my father.

One Sunday, we left home with our lunch boxes and water bottles and caught the bus to Chandigarh. On our way we checked our list. My father said, "Ok, let's get down at sector 17 and visit the nearest companies which are in sector 35. I still remember it was the month of December in 2004. We reached one of IT companies located in sector 35.

As we tried to enter the main gate of the company, the security guard stopped us with his outstretched hand and asked, "Yes Sir, who do you want to meet and for what purpose?"

I said, "We want to meet someone from the software department of this company. We have come to enrol for summer training."

The guard relented, "Ok, just enter your name, contact number and address in this register. Take this visitor's pass, go to reception and tell the person sitting there the same thing. They'll tell you what to do."

We reached the reception. A girl aged twenty or twenty three was sitting there. She was wearing a lot of makeup and looked very attractive. It was a small company. There were five small cabins and ten air-conditioned cubicles. The only sound one could hear was of typing on keyboards. I could see software engineers concentrating hard, staring at their computers and trying to find solutions to their technical problems.

The receptionist asked my father, "Yes Sir, how can I help you?"

We told her why we were there. She said, "Sir, at present, we're not planning to provide training to any fresher. But you can leave your resume here. We'll contact you in future if we have any such requirement." I knew in my heart that no one would contact me and it was just a polite way of saying goodbye to us. I left my resume and contact number with the lady and slowly walked out of the office with my father.

I spoke to myself, "How lucky this receptionist is. At least she's working somewhere and is in a position to tell people like us, 'Sorry we can't do anything for you. Better luck next time.' To top it all, she's even paid to say all this!"

We visited the next company in sector 34. As luck would have it, I got a chance to sit for the written test they were taking to select freshers for training. It was a walk in test. I cleared the test and got in to the second round for interviews. I had already read on the internet how one should face interviews so I was prepared for it.

I walked into the room with my resume. A very shrewd young lady conducted my interview. I greeted her and gave her my resume. She scanned it and said, "So you have done the advance Java course. Tell me about the features of high level language and then some features about the object oriented programming system - OOPS."

I answered confidently. We had an argument about some technical terms and finally the interview came to an end after forty five minutes.

I came out of room and my father asked me, "My great warrior, how was your interview?"

"The interview was great, Dad. We argued a lot. The interviewer was technically weak so I argued with her on some technical terms."

"My dear, you should never be aggressive in any interview."

"Dad, how could I agree with her when she was saying something totally incorrect? But I know she will select me as I was able to answer all their questions confidently. But you know what Dad? If they select me, I'll think twice before joining this company even though this company is bigger than the one we had visited earlier.

I asked them if they would pay a stipend during the training period. They said they wouldn't as they don't give regular training. They said they would assign one topic and we could prepare the software at home. "You can visit us at the end of each month to take inputs. After six months, we'll give you a certificate to the effect that you have completed your training," they told me.

"Dad, I don't want to waste six months only for the sake of a training certificate. It is the beginning of my career. I want to work at a place where I can gain some knowledge and experience which will help me in future."

My father reassured me, "Ok, if you aren't satisfied, then we can visit the remaining companies."

"Thanks Dad for all your support. But it's two o'clock now and I'm feeling hungry. Let's sit somewhere and have our lunch."

We looked for a place in the market at sector 35 where we could sit and eat our lunch. Finally we found a big tree with a bench under it. Both of us sat on the bench. I opened my lunch box. My mother had packed chapattis, pooris with potato bhaji, sliced onions and green chillies. It smelt heavenly. My father could never resist home-made food. And he simply loved the food cooked by my mother. We started eating lunch and within half an hour we had finished our meal. A cow, a common sight in Indian market places, saw the food and ambled towards us. My father gave some of the chapattis to the cow. After lunch we drank water and sat there for a while. A vendor was selling papri chaat at a distance and though I wasn't really hungry, my mouth started watering looking at my favourite snack.

My father understood I was really keen to have it and asked me, "My dear, do you want to eat it?"

"Yes, please."

My father went and bought a full plate for me.

"I know Dad, you also love papri chaat that's why you bought it. You're very clever," I told him playfully and we burst into laughter.

After resting for a few minutes, we hired a rickshaw and reached the market at Mohali Phase-7. A small IT company was located there but it looked more like a shop. It was the same company that had visited my institute for campus placements. We stood at the entrance and heard an employee fighting with his boss for his salary. He was shouting and abusing his boss, "You ******, either give me my last three months' salary pending with you or I will call the police."

My father and I looked at each other in surprise. My father said, "People in this company are obviously not getting their salary, how will they teach you? Let's go somewhere else." It is said -the first impression is the last impression – and sure enough, it made us leave that place in a minute.

There was one more company on the ground floor of the same building. I read the name of the company and told my father, "I think this must be an IT company. Let's go in and talk to someone."

My father and I entered the office. The door was open and we looked in. In one corner there was a bunch of wires, several routers and a CPU (must have been a server) that was blinking. There were five PCs and at the other end, there was a big leather chair and big glass table that seemed to be obviously for the boss. There was only one air conditioner in the window but it was powerful enough to cool that small room which was in such a mess that it didn't at all look like an IT company.

"Dad, I think someone has recently opened this company in the hope that it will turn into a big business in the near future," I voiced my thoughts.

There was one more room next to the first room. From a crack in the door, we saw it also had a few more PCs, a cupboard and a few boxes lying against the wall. I could see they had just unpacked the hardware and arranged it in that room. My father knocked on the door two times and asked, "Anyone there?"

Suddenly a tall, dark and handsome man dressed in blue jeans and a checked shirt came out. He was strong and masculine and he exuded the very familiar heady denim talc scent that any woman would find attractive. While his fragrance still pervaded my senses, he asked my father, "Yes Sir, how can I help you?"

My father asked, "Is this an IT company?"

"Yes Sir. We run both IT and research work from here but today, our boss is not in the office. What can I do for you, Sir?"

"Would you be providing six months training to freshers in information technology?" my father asked.

"Sir, I am into research work and I have no idea if the boss will permit this kind of training or not."

"Could you please tell us when can we meet him?"

"Sure. I'll call him and you can talk to him."

"What's your name?" my father asked.

"My name's Jaison.," Mr. Denim Talc said.

"This is my daughter Naina and she is looking for a six month training in an IT company," my father informed while introducing me to that guy.

Jaison took out his black Nokia phone from his pocket his fingers typing fast on its keypad. "Morning Sir, How are you?" he paused for a moment, "Sir, there's a gentleman here who would like to talk to you about training for his daughter."

He put his boss on hold and told my father, "Please talk to him. He'd like to have a word with you."

I snatched the phone from his hands and started talking excitedly.

"Hello Sir, I'm from Yamuna Nagar and I've done my MCA and as per our curriculum, we have to complete six months training in some IT company. On the basis of the training certificate, we get a score in the sixth semester. Do you provide such trainings?"

"Yes, we can provide you with training. I am on my way to Mohali. I'll be reaching there in fifteen minutes. If you can wait for me then we can interview you and decide further," said the boss from the other side.

"Ok, Sir. I'm waiting for you," I replied happily.

I returned the phone to Jaison. My fingers brushed his and I felt as though an electric current had gone through me. My father thanked him.

I didn't know it then but destiny was stepping in from this moment of my life which was about to take a different turn from here.

The boss arrived in twenty minutes. He greeted us and asked us to sit down and ordered two cups of tea from a stall near his office.

I gave my CV to the boss. Flipping through its pages, he scanned it carefully. He then started interviewing me. He asked me around twelve to fifteen questions on the computer language Java. I was able to answer almost eleven questions confidently.

"Ok, so your technical knowledge is pretty good. We will provide you with training. But this will be a training that is paid for. You will have to pay a thousand rupees per month to us and if you perform well during this period, then we will also offer you a job. You can join us from January and we will also arrange accommodation for you."

My father and I were overjoyed, "Thanks a lot. We will contact you after we have a final discussion at home on your offer."

We reached sector-17 bus stand and bought our tickets for a bus to Yamuna Nagar. After settling down in our seats, my father and I started our discussion.

"I didn't know that my daughter is so intelligent and confident. Though we don't have any contacts, you've cleared two interviews because you're so capable. I'm proud of you, my dear little Naina. Now you have two options to select from and I'm feeling relaxed. It's up to you to decide which company you want to join. "Dad, I'm a fresher. It's important that I learn as much as I can. So it's better to join a small company where I can get regular training. Not like the one which will just provide me with only a training certificate. This learning experience will help me get a better job in future. People like us who have passed out from small institutes have to struggle a lot. But I appreciate the fact Dad that you've supported me."

After completing my fifth semester, I started preparing for my sixth semester. Finally it was time to leave Yamuna Nagar. When destiny has planned something for you then everything and every person will be in your favour. This was happening with me also.

My father said, "It's the first time you're going out of your hometown. I am allowing you to do this because you are a bright, intelligent and ambitious girl. I want to give you a chance. If possible, I'll send your mother to Chandigarh. She'll stay with you so that you may not feel lonely there."

"Dad, don't send Mom with me. What will you do without her? She's the only one who takes care of everything at home. You won't be able to manage anything at home without her. I know you don't want to leave me alone but let me manage by myself."

"My dear girl, never let us down! Let us always feel proud of you." Finally, he expressed what was worrying him the most. I had expected this.

Everything moved very quickly after this. Mother packed all my clothes in two bags. She also packed a bucket, a mug, a soap case, some pickles, some sweets and home-made snacks, along with my bedding.

There was a feeling of sadness when I left home and everything that was familiar to me. Saying good bye to my mother was especially difficult.

My father and I caught a bus to Chandigarh. It was difficult to carry so many luggages. My bedding went on the top of the bus. Though the bus was very crowded, my father managed to adjust the two big bags under our seats. In two hours we reached Chandigarh. We got down at

Kisaan Bhawan and hired an auto rickshaw to reach Mohali phase-7 market.

We met the boss and he gave us the address of a paying guest accommodation that was at a walking distance of ten minutes from the office. My father and I asked a few people and found the house.

Chandigarh is a planned city, as is Mohali. Every colony and sector is well developed and structured. There is something special about Chandigarh. People here have a good standard of living even if some of them are not well educated. They eat well and live well because one person from every family has gone abroad to earn a better livelihood. The dollars that they send to their family back home in Chandigarh enhances the standard of living of the family. This fact appealed to me a lot.

The paying guest house was a pink coloured, three storeyed building. There was a small lawn at one side and a park in front of the house which belonged to the housing society. We met the owner. She was a young, married, Punjabi lady living with her in-laws, her two children and her husband on the ground floor. Her husband had his own gym and was a gym instructor there. Harpreet Kaur, as we learnt her name was, greeted us. She obviously knew about us as my boss had informed her in advance about our visit. She took me to my room on the first floor.

It was big and spacious and beautifully designed. There were three bedrooms, one big hall and a kitchen. Two girls were staying in one room. I was given a room which had two folding beds and one bathroom. The bathroom was tastefully designed and had everything in matching red and white.

Harpreet Kaur said, "I charge two thousand five hundred rupees per month from each girl and these are my rules." She started, much like a sergeant, while we stood to attention:

"No girl should use an electric iron as it increases the electricity bill. If you have brought an iron with you, then please give it to me. I'll return it to you when you leave this PG.

I provide three meals a day - breakfast, lunch and dinner. My menu is fixed and it won't change for anyone. I cook only vegetarian food.

I don't give fruits. If you want to eat anything extra, you'll have to buy it yourself.

Your floor doesn't have television. So everyone will watch television only in my hall.

You can't watch TV after ten at night.

Everyone should come back home by nine o'clock.

After nine o'clock, I will lock the main door from inside and if you're late then you'll have to stay outside.

You'll get all the meals at a fixed time - breakfast at eight, lunch at one and dinner at half past eight. You can either have tea or a glass of milk along with breakfast.

If on any day you don't want to eat at home, then you will have to inform me in advance so that I don't waste food.

No boys are allowed inside my PG.

If you have a boyfriend, make sure you don't meet him anywhere in this colony as it may ruin my reputation.

You can't wear indecent clothes at my place.

If you go out during the weekend, you'll have to inform me where you're going.

On the very first day you'll have to give me your father's name, home address, telephone number, your office/college address and contact number."

I felt almost breathless hearing her rattle off her long list of rules.

My father said, "I can understand, Mrs. Harpreet, it is not easy to run a girls' PG. It's such a big responsibility for you, so definitely there should be some rules to maintain discipline. I'm very happy to have met you. By the way, my girl is a very good and sincere child. She won't bother you at all. Please take good care of her."

Harpreet Kaur felt proud of herself and reassured my father in chaste Punjabi, "Tussi Chinta na karo ji. Ethhey sariyan kudiyan meri hai. Onada thyan rakh di haan mein (Don't worry! Here, all the girls are like my daughters and I take care of them)."

I kept my luggage in my new room and paid the rent to Madam Harpreet. All PG owners have one thing in common - when you pay them rent, they behave as if you are the sweetest person on this earth. Harpreet said lovingly, "its lunch time. Come on, I'll give you food. She called out to the other girls too, "Girls, come downstairs for your meal."

She served me one small bowl of curry, curd and hot chapattis.

I didn't like the taste of the food but still I ate it as I had no other choice. I was already missing my mother's food. My mother was a good cook and always served us delicious food. At home, I had never eaten less than two curries, salad, chapattis and a sweet dish for every meal.

It was time to say good bye to my father. He said, "We'll miss you dear. It's the first time that you're away from home. You'll miss us and might want to talk to us many times. Here, keep this. I've bought a second hand mobile phone for you. Get a prepaid connection today itself from the market and give us your number when it gets activated. Visit us every weekend and you'll feel happy. Call me whenever you need me."

My father took a long last look at me, hugged me and was gone in a second. He left for Yamuna Nagar immediately.

I made my bed and put all my belongings in the cupboard. I sat on the bed and stared at the walls as I had nothing to do. It was a weekday and all my PG mates were at college. I started feeling lonely. I was missing home and my mother and the rest of the family. I changed my clothes and decided to go to office.

I told Harpreet, "Aunty, I'm going to office and I'll come back in the evening."

I reached office and met all the staff members .There were six boys and one girl. Two other boys who were of my age group, had joined as trainees. All the trainees introduced themselves to each other.

The boss assigned a project to the trainees. We were asked to design a website for a property portal within one month. Out of the existing six employees, only two were from IT while the others were involved in research work. This company had been started by two people in partnership. One was the head of the IT department and the other was the head of the research department.

The research team was led by Jaison. He was the only person I had met when I came here for the first time for the interview. I didn't know then that all the boys liked my presence in the office. I suppose that a good looking girl in the team always gets a lot of attention from her colleagues. Everyone tries to approach her and find some excuse to talk to her.

The research team and the IT team sat in separate rooms. After every two hours, the employees would order tea from a small tea stall down the road and the bill was paid monthly. In the absence of the boss the employees would use his landline phone to talk to their friends and families.

On the first day itself, I was asked to prepare the layout of a website on paper and give a presentation the following day.

I left for the day on a good note, went back to the PG and met all my PG roommates. They were four girls who were doing their MBA from a college in Mohali. All of them were beautiful Punjabi girls who had come from villages in Punjab. Exactly at half past eight, the bell was rung to let us know that dinner was ready. All the girls started talking at once, "God only knows what aunty has cooked today. Every week it's the same menu. We're fed up of this tasteless food. But what can we do?" I was the eldest of all. They told me in Punjabi, "Didi, you're new here, gradually you'll come to know how many restrictions there are in this PG digs."

All the girls reached the dining hall. My roommate Meena took off the lid of the bowl kept on the dining table and took a whiff of whatever had been cooked for the day. I could also smell the rich Punjabi kadi.

Meena said, "Aunty, thank God you have cooked Punjabi kadi and rice today!" She whispered in my ears, "It's your first day and Aunty wants to impress you. So she's cooked her best dish."

All of us ate the food in front of us. I enjoyed the food more because it was spiced with my roommate's college gossip. After dinner, one girl picked up the TV remote and switched on the television. We started watching the 'Miss Punjab' beauty pageant. After half an hour, around half past ten, aunty shouted at all of us, "Now switch it off and go back to your rooms. Don't forget to switch off the lights of the staircase and your rooms before sleeping."

We grimaced, obediently switched off the television set and went back to our rooms. Before sleeping, we huddled on one bed and started our gossip session. Suddenly, we heard the loud voices of Aunty and her husband.

I signalled everyone to keep quiet and said, "Shhh, keep quiet for a minute, someone's fighting downstairs".

Addressing me as an elder sister, Meena said, "Didi, it happens every day. Uncle and Aunty fight every single day."

"But why?" I asked.

"Didi do you know that Uncle is having has an extra marital affair? That's why Aunty looks so frustrated all the time."

"Oh, that's bad! I am feeling so sorry for Aunty."

After that long gossip session, everyone said good night to each other and went to bed.

Meena and I went to our room and the two other girls slept in another room.

I switched off the lights. It was winter. We cocooned ourselves in our quilts and snuggled in bed. I was missing my family, especially my mother and my father, and felt a deep longing to talk to them. But I didn't have a phone connection yet so I couldn't do anything about it.

I was trying to fall asleep in that unfamiliar place. Suddenly I heard a lot of giggling from the bed next to mine. It was Meena. She had covered her face with her quilt and was talking to someone on her cell phone.

I understood that Meena had a boyfriend. She was speaking in Punjabi with him. She even started kissing her cell phone. It seemed a little crazy and made me feel very uncomfortable. I tried to reason with myself that people in love would behave that way. I heard her whisper in Punjabi, "Darling, we'll have two kids - one will be Manpreet and other one will be Karanpreet." I could not control myself and muffled my laughter in my quilt. She talked to him till one in the night.

Next morning, Aunty rang the bell for breakfast. Everyone reached the dining table. Aunty gave everyone paranthas with butter and tea or milk according to what they wanted.

She asked, "At what time did you girls sleep yesterday? I saw that in the last room lights were switched on till half past eleven."

"Aunty, we were studying till late in the night so the lights were on," Meena replied smartly.

I looked at the other girls and smiled. Meena whispered, "Didi, actually Aunty is wondering if we were awake while they were fighting. She thinks we don't know what happens in her house."

After finishing breakfast, every one said goodbye to Aunty and we left. I reached office, took my seat and switched on my desktop. Jaison came to the IT department and greeted everyone. He said loudly "Hi Naina!"

Deeply conscious of his presence, I replied softly, "Hi Jaison." Then everyone got back to their work.

After some time, our boss Mr. Manjeet Singh asked me to make the presentation on the white board. People from both departments came to see my presentation. I explained the design on the white board with the help of flowcharts and diagrams.

Mr. Singh said, "Well done, Naina! Can you think of some more inputs to this design and tell me now?" I thought for five minutes and came out with a few more innovative ideas.

He looked happy, "It looks good to me."

Then I asked everyone, "Do you have any questions or suggestions?" There was complete silence for one minute and then Manjeet Singh said, "Since there are no more questions, you should start working on this property portal with your colleagues from now onwards."

One week passed quickly and by this time I got a prepaid phone connection. One day, I was alone in the PG and I started missing my family very badly. I called up my parents.

My parents were very happy to hear from me. My mother sounded tearful, "How are you dear? Are you able to adjust in the new environment? Do you miss us?"

I could not answer her back and started crying bitterly. "Mom, I miss all of you. Now I understand how difficult it is to stay away from your family. I don't know how children who live in hostels spend so many years without their families. I miss home, your home cooked food, Dad and Priyanshu very much."

My mother handed over the phone to my father.

"Hello, my dear! Now, now why are you crying? Don't cry, please. It happens with everyone. I remember when I was transferred to Hissar, I felt the same way. But after some days, you'll get used to this new lifestyle. Priyanshu also felt sad when he joined the hostel for the first time but now he feels quite at home in the hostel and enjoys life with his friends. You should make friends too and together you can go window shopping or for a morning walk."

"Dad, I have very nice PG mates but they all are from the same college so they are very friendly with each other. They're not of my age group so I feel lonely and out of place when they talk about their college and friends."

Dad gave the phone to Priyanshu, "Didi, why you are crying? It's the weekend now. If you have no friends there then why don't you come to Yamuna Nagar?"

I said, "But how will I come alone?"

Priyanshu said, "Listen to me carefully. I've seen every corner of Chandigarh with my friends, so I can tell you how you can get a bus for Yamuna Nagar. You should first get a rickshaw to the nearest circle and then catch a local Punjab Roadways bus that goes to sector 17 bus stand. After reaching sector 17, ask at the booth from where you can get a direct bus to Yamuna Nagar. If by chance you don't get a direct bus, you can get into any bus that goes to Ambala. When you reach Ambala, get down at Ambala Cantt bus stand, opposite the railway station and from there, you can easily get a bus for Yamuna Nagar."

I smiled, "Thanks, Priyanshu. I'll pack my luggage right now and I'll reach home by evening."

I packed a small bag with two sets of clothes and reached sector 17 bus stand. Fortunately, I got a direct bus to Yamuna Nagar. Within two hours, I reached home.

When my mother opened the door, my eyes filled with tears. She opened her arms and I hugged her tight. My father also came running to see me. He hugged me and started laughing loudly. He said, "Hey, look at my daughter. She's crying. She always wanted to stay away from home but now she's crying."

My father took me in his arms and consoled me and made me laugh by making a few lame jokes. I passed the weekend joyfully with my family and left for Chandigarh on Monday early in the morning.

My mother gave me an extra bag. She had stuffed it with homemade snacks. Back in office, I shared the snacks with everyone.

Jaison was very fond of eating. He finished one big jar of snacks all by himself. I got worried and immediately went back to my PG to leave my bags in the room. I hid the snacks in the cupboard behind the dressing table. Thanks to my mother, the whole cupboard was full of snacks now.

I had my lunch and came back to office. Gradually, I became friends with everyone in office. Jaison was more mature than the others and being a team leader, he never spoke too much with me. It seemed that he always wanted to maintain a distance between us.

After one month our boss Mr. Manjeet Singh invited all of us to a pizza party to celebrate his birthday. Jaison was the organiser. He invited everyone and asked me, "Hey, aren't you coming with us to the party tomorrow?"

I said, "No, I may not come tomorrow. It's the weekend and today evening I'm going to my aunt. She lives here in Chandigarh."

Jaison didn't like my refusal but he did not express it. I understood that he expected me to be present at this party. He said, "Ok, as you wish."

My colleague Paramjeet asked me, "Why did you say no? You should come with us and enjoy at the party. You can go to your aunt's place after the party. Don't worry I'll drop you on my scooty."

I thought for a second and accepted her offer, "Ok Paramjeet, if you drop me then its fine."

The following day, all of us reached Pizza Hut in sector 26. We ordered four big pizzas out of which two were vegetarian and two, non-vegetarian. I was eating pizza for the first time in my life. In small towns, people usually prefer homemade food to fast food. They haven't developed a taste for fast food as yet. Jaison and Manjeet Singh ordered a big jug of chilled beer. Within a few minutes, the waiter brought us the pizza we had ordered. It was a hot pan pizza. The waiter cautioned, "Madam, please be careful as the pan is very hot."

I observed how the others were taking pizza from the pan with a big spatula. I did the same. I was wondering how I should eat the pizza – should I eat with my hands or with a fork and knife? I saw a few people eat it with a knife and fork while the others ate with their hands. I tried to eat it with a fork and knife but could not cut it. I felt embarrassed. I looked here and there and started eating it with my hands. The boys were busy drinking beer and gossiping. I didn't like the taste of pizza as it had a lot of cheese and I had never eaten so much cheese in my life. Somehow I managed to eat only one piece.

Paramjeet noticed my pained expression and said, "Hey, why have you stopped eating? Take one more piece. It tastes awesome."

I passed the pan to the other side and said, "Paramjeet, I've finished. I'm not so fond of pizza."

"Oh really! You're the first person who doesn't like pizza. It's really very tasty. Once you develop a taste for it, you'll love it."

Soon Jaison was so drunk that he started blabbering out his secrets, "Sir, she said no to my proposal. On top of that, she invited me to her wedding! I'm such a fool. I liked her so much."

I was shocked. I kept looking at his face. The other boys laughed and told the girls not to be shocked. "It happens when guys are drunk. They talk nonsense but they speak the truth."

I asked Paramjeet softly, "Did he ever have a girlfriend? Is he missing her?"

"I don't know much about it. But I know he had a crush on someone in his previous company."

Everyone was in a jolly mood. Manjeet Singh said, "Now each one of you will either sing or tell us a joke or play 'antakshari'. Come on guys, its party time! So we'll start one by one."

It started with Paramjeet. She told us a joke and everyone laughed. Then Jaison sang a sad song, as he was missing the person he'd had a crush on. Manjeet Singh consoled him by pressing his shoulders.

When it was my turn, I sang a song from one of the latest Hindi movies. Everyone clapped. The party went on for one more hour. Then we left happily for home.

After two months, the research department and the IT department were merged. We started sitting in one room. The other room became like a junk yard and the office started looking more like a store room. My interaction with Jaison started with small fights.

One day I was creating some flow diagrams on my system. Jaison looked at my system and tried to attract everyone's attention by saying, "Hey, look at her. She comes here to draw balloons on her screen." He laughed and clapped.

I stared at him and said, "Shut up. It is beyond you. You won't understand this anyway. Don't disturb me."

"Hey Haryana hurricane, don't threaten me. I'm not afraid of you. Why do you get irritated when I speak the truth?" He tried to irritate me even more.

"Do you know you're not even a human being? You're like petrol-inflammable. You can easily ignite a calm environment," I gave it back to him.

"Are you even aware of the way you speak? It's as if you're beating the other person with a stick rather than having a normal conversation," he replied.

I was furious, "You overweight oaf, don't mess with me. I'm from Haryana and I'm proud of that. We're bold people and not scared of anyone. Tell me, where are you from?"

"I was born and brought up in Chandigarh but my parents are from Kerala. Basically, I'm a Malayalee(south Indian) but I like Punjab very much," he replied.

The others started betting on our fight. "Come on guys, let's see who wins - Punjab or Haryana?"

"Shut up everyone. I love Punjab too. All my friends are Punjabi. But this Jaison irritates me a lot. This South Indian Malayalee boy wants to fight with me. But he'll never win," I said feeling irritated.

Jaison said, "No one can defeat me."

I retorted with a lot of rancour in my voice, "Shut up."

Day by day our fights became worse and it became a source of entertainment for the others. I started calling him "Petrol".

One day I came to know that Jaison was feeling disturbed and not talking to anyone in the office. I asked his friend, Aslam, what the reason could be.

Aslam informed me, "We haven't got our salaries for the last two months. Our boss is going through a financial crisis. He started this company in order to do big business but it seems to us that it's not working. He doesn't even have money to pay our salaries. Jaison lost his father two years back. His father was a diabetic patient. After his father passed away, he has taken over his father's responsibilities. He's now a father figure for his younger sister. She's studying in Bangalore and he has to send five thousand rupees every month to his sister for her expenses. Over and above, Jaison has to pay sixty thousand rupees as tuition fees every year to his sister's college. Now he doesn't have money to send to his sister so he is feeling disturbed."

Jaison was sitting on his chair lost in his thoughts. I pushed his chair from the back and said, "Hi, how are you?"

"Hi," his reply came back with a weak smile.

"I know why you're so depressed. If you need any help, I'm here to help you. My father sends me five thousand rupees per month for my expenses. I can save some money and I can give it to you for your sister."

"Thanks, you're kind and thoughtful. But I don't take money from anyone. Don't worry, I'll manage."

My heart went out to him and I really wanted to help him. But I also didn't want to make him feel helpless. I knew he was brave and would manage things on his own. So I left him alone. From that day onwards, I had a lot of respect in my heart for Jaison though we continued to quarrel over small things.

The following month, our boss somehow managed to give salaries to all his employees. All of us were happy.

"So now are you happy, Mr. Petrol?"

"Yes, I am! Do you want to have tea and samosas?" he offered.

"Sure! I know you're a big time eater. Every hour you need something to eat and after every two hours you go to the toilet. I tell you, you're no less than an elephant."

Aslam laughed. All three of us went down the road to have tea and samosas at a tea stall. Aslam and Jaison were good friends. Each time Jaison and I fought in office, all the others would have a good laugh at our expense. Aslam, Jaison and I always went out together to the tea stall, juice corner or just to eat bananas with a dash of salt. There we would have long sessions just gossiping. After we had eaten, Aslam and Jaison would always ask me to go back to office. One day I asked both of them, "Why is it that we come together but I always go back alone? Do you guys share your secrets when I'm not here? Is this what your friendship is all about?"

Aslam laughed out loud and said, "Baby, we ask you to leave because we smoke. You seem to be forgetting one thing. When we come back later, we always give you some mouth freshener or mint candy which we buy and eat to hide the foul cigarette smell. That's why you've never come to know the truth."

I made a face and started shouting at them. "Do you guys know smoking is injurious to health? Jaison, you've lost your father and now you're trying to finish yourself. Have you ever thought what will happen to your family if something happens to you? Imagine your loved ones crying over your death. And you, Aslam? You already look like a dried up tree. Keep on smoking and no girl will ever look at you. You'll remain a bachelor throughout your life. Remember, girls don't like chain smokers."

After this long lecture which I delivered like a parrot, I left them to themselves. A few minutes later, they came back to office and apologised to me. Jaison said, "I hadn't really thought about it. I promise that I'll give up smoking. But it can't happen all of a sudden. It'll take time."

"Ok. This sounds good," I replied while hitting the keys hard on my keyboard.

A few days later, I got a phone call from one of my old friends called Leena.

I was excited to hear her voice when the phone rang, "Hi Leena, how are you? It's been so long since I last spoke to you. Tell me, where are you?"

"I'm in Chandigarh. I got your number from your mother."

I said, "Great. We're both in the same city. Let's plan to meet one weekend."

"Ok, I live in sector 32. Come to my place one day and stay with me. We'll plan something."

I said. "Sounds great! So this Saturday I'm coming to your place. Text me your address."

The following day I told Jaison, "Petrol, do you know why I'm so happy today?'

Jaison looked at me lovingly and asked, "Ok, tell me why?"

"Yesterday I got a call from my childhood friend. I came to know that she's here in Chandigarh. I am going to meet her this weekend," I said.

Jaison added, "Wow! That's great. So you'll have a rocking weekend."

One week passed. On Saturday I got ready, informed my care taker that I was going to visit my friend and told her that I would be back by Sunday evening.

I reached sector 32 and met Leena. Unlike me, Leena had been living independently in a two roomed flat. Therefore, there were no rules to be followed or restrictions to be observed. She was paying a rent of three thousand five hundred rupees. I, on the other hand, was a paying guest.

I looked at her flat and said, "Wow, I feel so free and independent here. I can actually smell freedom."

Leena said, "I can understand how you feel because you're staying in a PG. But you know, I have to cook, clean and look after everything myself whereas, you don't have any such problems."

"Yes, I know. Everything has its pros and cons."

"Anyway, tell me, what's going on in your life other than your training?"

"Well, now I'm enjoying office life. I have two good friends there. They are boys. Though I fight with one of them a lot, I enjoy with them too."

"Hmm, madam, be careful! You'll never come to know when these fights turn into love and then my dear," she cautioned me, "you'll face a lot of problems."

I remained silent for a few seconds and then changed the topic.

"Ok, tell me, what's your plan for today?'

"Get ready, first we'll go to sector 22 to do some fancy shopping and then in the evening, we'll go to the sector-17 market."

Leena and I dressed up in our best outfits, sprayed deodorants and splashed perfume liberally on ourselves and hired a rickshaw to reach sector 22.

On reaching the market in sector 22, both of us went crazy. This market was full of fashionable clothes, jewellery, shoes and all kind of girlie things. We spent three hours in the market and shopped together. After shopping, we were happy and excited as though we had won the world cup!

Then we hired a rickshaw to take us to sector-17. When we reached there, we realised that we had become really famished. We felt totally drained of energy.

Leena said, "There are many shops here selling aloo chaat. Let's have one plate each of chaat and gol gappas. Then we'll have ice cream."

We ate to our heart's content. Then we roamed around for a bit. In Chandigarh, sector-17 is considered to be a famous and beautiful market. To me, it seemed like a European market. It had a big open space in the middle and then there were shops on all four sides.

There were beautiful Punjabi girls wearing bright coloured dresses. The newly married girls wearing red chooras looked stunning. Punjabi girls enhance the beauty of Chandigarh. We saw couples sitting on benches under trees sharing ice creams.

There were many shops selling aloo chaat, ice cream and burgers which attracted people of every age group. Girls and boys were walking here and there in groups. I saw many well-endowed Punjabi ladies getting down from their expensive cars in the parking area and walking towards the shops with their big purses. In the middle of the market, there was a live band and a vocalist who made that evening particularly romantic.

I also observed some spoilt young boys misbehaving with girls. A few naughty boys were following a girl and trying to take her photograph from the back.

Leena and I found a place to sit down. We kept on gossiping and chatting. It was half past ten in the night now when we thought of going back home.

Our weekend went by and when I joined office back on Monday, I found Jaison surrounded by all his colleagues. I came by to check what was happening. I saw him staring at one girl's photograph on his desktop. He was telling Aslam, "Look at her; she is so simple and attractive. I like such Indian beauties. She is a Keralite Christian. My mother wants me to marry her."

I listened to everything and quietly went back to my seat. The whole day I did not speak to anyone. I didn't even eat my lunch.

Jaison and Aslam came to me, "Hey, we are going out to drink juice. Come on, get up and join us."

I said, "No, I'm not feeling well, I am going back to my PG. I want to take rest." I left office early, reached my PG and took a shower. Under the shower, I cried loudly and felt very low. My phone kept ringing.

After half an hour, I came out of the bathroom and saw that there were twenty missed calls from Jaison. I threw the phone on my bed. It rang again. This time I took the call and said, "Hello."

It was Jaison, "Hello, where were you? Why didn't you pick up the phone? What's happened to you? Come to office now and we will go out for coffee."

I hung up after telling him, "No, I won't be coming, I'm not feeling well. I'd like to take rest."

After a few minutes, my phone rang again. Aslam called me up and said, "Don't say anything and come to office. We're waiting for you."

I had to go to office. Jaison and Aslam were waiting for me. Jaison looked in to my eyes and asked, "I can read your eyes. Tell me what's happened or I'll open my mouth and tell everyone the truth."

I looked away. There was a lot of turmoil inside me. Leena's words, "Sweet fights turn into deep love," kept echoing in my ears.

I told Aslam, "Aslam tell him I'm missing my family very much, so I just want to go back home."

Jaison said, "Today when you came to office in the morning there was nothing like that but now you say that you're missing your family. You can't tell me lies. I know you very well, baby. Come on, look into my eyes and say that you are actually missing your family."

I looked down and did not look in to his eyes as I was bewildered by my thoughts.

Jaison took my hand in his hands and said, "I know you didn't like it when I praised that girl and set her picture as my wallpaper."

I tried to pretend, "Are you mad? There is nothing like that!" Aslam left us alone.

Jaison smiled and said, "I read your eyes when you left the office early today. I wanted to know your feelings for me. So I thought of a way. I only praised that girl in front of you to make you feel jealous. Otherwise, I had no intention of hurting you."

I asked him, "What did you want to know?"

Jaison asked me, "Tell me one thing honestly. Do you like me?"

I was shocked. It was as if someone had caught me stealing money from a temple.

I stammered, "No, umm, it's not like that. You're just a good friend."

Jaison and I were silent for a few seconds. I looked up and found him staring at me.

Suddenly, he broke the silence, "I like you very much and I am not a liar like you. I long to come to office every morning, just to see you. And my heart feels heavy when you leave early. I like our fights and I like to spend time with you. I think I started liking you from the very first time you came here with your father. I was taken aback to see such beauty. Our fights made us grow close and gradually, we became friends. After you became my friend, I liked you as a person too because you're so down to earth, you love your parents, you are so clean hearted, very ambitious and such a hardworking lady. I feel you're a woman of substance."

While listening to Jaison my eyes filled with tears. I had long suppressed my feelings for him. There was a lump in my throat and my voice became heavy. I finally managed to speak, "Yes, I like you very much. In fact, I love you. Today my heart broke when you praised that girl and said that you want to marry her. You are so sensible, caring, adorable and most importantly, you don't show off. You are mature and I like you very much."

Jaison's eyes filled with tears too. He took me gently by my shoulders and said, "Dear, we will have to kill the feelings we have for each other. We cannot take this relationship forward because I'm a Christian and you're a Hindu. I belong to a Malayalee family from Kerala while you belong to a Hindu family. Our families will never accept this relationship. Both families live in two different worlds. You are an ambitious girl and you have a long way to go. I don't want your family to thwart your bright career because of me. I have so many responsibilities on my shoulders. I can never think about starting a relationship or marrying anyone because I first have to take care of my younger sister. I've lost my father, so I'll have to take care of her studies and her marriage. I don't want to lose my focus in life."

I kept my head on Jaison's shoulder and sobbed. I said, "You're right. My family is very conservative and in my family, no girl has the right to go against her parents' wishes. Till now, in my family, no girl has dared to fall in love. I am also scared of starting a relationship. We'll always be friends and nothing more than that."

Jaison said, "Yes, my sweetheart. I always want to see you happy. You can get married to a good guy later. There is no point in starting a meaningless relationship and crying over it later."

From that day onwards, Jaison and I never fought with each other. We stopped looking into each other's eyes. We didn't want our feelings to surface. We just spoke to each other formally. But, however hard we tried to push back our thoughts and feelings for each other, it would rear its head even more powerfully, if only to disconcert us. We tried to maintain a distance from each other but once in a while during the day, we secretly stole glances at each other while eating, laughing or talking to others.

One day, Aslam told Jaison, "Man, I know that you love Naina. Then why don't you just let it come out? You are doing injustice to yourself. Respect the feelings and the love you feel for her. You both are killing yourselves day by day."

4

Chunnu and Nariyal

One night, I got a call from Jaison at around ten in the night. I could not stop myself and took the call.

"Hi dear, what were you doing?" Jaison said softly.

"I've had my dinner and I was going to sleep," I replied.

"Weren't you thinking about me?" he asked.

I kept quiet and my silence was enough to reveal everything.

Jaison said, "You're my sweetheart. I always think about you in my dreams. I'm feeling bad you're leaving for home tomorrow. I'll really miss you. I want to tell you everything today. When I saw you for the first time, I was attracted to your physical beauty - your height, your lips, your eyes and your hair. But I swear as time passed I started liking your inner beauty more than your outer beauty. You are my Chunnu."

I giggled hearing him say that. "Chunnu! Wow, that's such a cute name. But you, you're my Nariyal. This is my sweet name for you."

We talked through the night and our relationship took a new turn. We were closer to each other. Our conversation became naughty and flirtatious. We realised that we loved each other deeply and couldn't live without seeing each other.

It was four in the morning. I looked at the time and said, "Oh my God, it is four in the morning! Thank God no one from home tried my number, otherwise they would have wondered why my phone was busy in the middle of the night." I asked Jaison, "Where is your mom? Does she know that you've been talking to a girl for such a long time?"

Jaison said, "No, no. She doesn't know about it. She's sleeping in the other room. Ok my Chunnu, you should take some rest now. I'll come to pick you up at seven. Meet me on the road behind your PG."

I said, "Ok sweetheart, I'm going to sleep now". I slept as soon as my head touched the pillow.

I got up at half past six. My roommate asked me, "Sister, who were you talking to last night?"

I smiled and said, "Bye, I'm going home. Take care of yourself. I'll be back after three days."

Jaison dropped me at the bus stand. I got into the bus for Yamuna Nagar and looked for a window seat. I looked at Jaison standing there and we smiled at each other. Jaison came closer to the window and kissed my hand. "I'll miss you my Chunnu." Now the bus was about to leave. He asked me, "Hey, do you have anything to eat and drink during the journey?"

I said, "No. But don't worry. I'll manage."

He didn't listen but walked fast to a small kiosk at the bus stand and bought a packet of chips and a cold drink for me. As the bus left the depot, we kept looking at each other till we went out of each other's sight.

All through the two hours of my journey, I kept thinking about the previous night's conversation over the phone. I felt as if my life had taken a completely different turn. I was falling in love and I knew that it would never be accepted by anyone in my family. I was so lost in my thoughts that I did not even realise that the bus had arrived at Yamuna Nagar. Suddenly, as the driver applied the brakes, I lurched forward and this sudden movement jolted me out of my wonderful reverie.

I met my mother when I reached home. She looked at me anxiously and asked, "Naina, why do you have dark circles under your eyes? Didn't you sleep well last night?"

I was scared. I said, "No Mom, actually I wasn't feeling well. I'll sleep now and I'll feel better."

While I was sleeping, Priyanshu picked up my cell phone and started using it. From childhood he had this habit of prying in my personal belongings like my cupboard, my books and now, even my phone. When I woke up, Priyanshu asked me, "Hey, I was using your phone and found that your last call lasted for six hours. Who on earth were you talking with for so long last night?"

I was scared again. I replied smartly, "Yesterday my school friend had called me after many years and we talked for a long time."

Priyanshu appeared to be satisfied with my answer. I took a deep breath. I was missing Jaison badly. In the night I went to the most isolated corner of our house - our store room and called him.

Jaison picked up the phone, "Hey, Chunnu how are you? I'm missing you so much. Come back soon."

I said, "Same here. I can't live without you. I am calling you secretly, almost like a thief. Hey, I better keep the phone now or my brother will suspect something. I just wanted to hear your voice. Bye. Sweet dreams, Nariyal. Love you sooooooo much." I blew kisses into the phone.

Three days passed and I was so happy that I was going back to Jaison. I reached Chandigarh on Monday morning. Jaison was there to receive me at Kisaan Bhawan. He dropped me on a road behind the PG and said, "Ok, bye sweetheart. It is only eight o'clock. I'll see you in the office at nine thirty."

I reached my PG, changed my clothes, ate breakfast and reached office before nine thirty.

I switched on my computer and started writing a programme using Java code. After one and a half hours, I looked at the clock on the wall and it was ten o'clock. I looked at the main door. I was longing to see Jaison. Suddenly I heard footsteps. Someone was coming upstairs. I felt happy. I heard a cheery "Hi" from the back. I turned around but it was Aslam. I was disappointed but I didn't show it. I smiled weakly and said, "Hi Aslam, how are you?"

"I'm fine, thanks. How was your visit? We missed you a lot. There was no one to fight with Jaison!" he added with a naughty look.

I said, "I enjoyed my stay at home and ate a lot of homemade food. My mother is a very good cook. I have brought some homemade gujiyas for all of you. I am waiting for Jaison. But Mr. Jaison is a VIP, why should he come on time? He is a big liar. He told me that he would meet me sharp at nine thirty in the office today. But look at him, he doesn't understand the one simple fact of life - time is money. He is so disorganised, he can never reach on time."

Aslam laughed but kept quiet.

Jaison sailed in at ten thirty and said a cheery "Hi" to all of us.

Aslam added, "Hi dude, best of luck!" Jaison raised his eyebrows and asked quizzically, "Best of luck, but for what?"

Aslam said, "Wait and see."

I did not respond to Jaison's greeting. I kept banging hard on my keyboard to show him that I had to complete a lot of work and that I didn't have a minute to even wish anyone. Jaison came closer to my seat and put his arms around me from the back and pressed ctrl+alt+delete on my keyboard, to lock my screen.

I got irritated and said, "Can't you see I'm working? I have a lot of work to do. I've promised to give the design and coding to the boss by the end of the day.

Jaison said, "Please come out with me and let's have tea together. Please, please, please."

I wanted to shout at him. So I got up and went out with him. While leaving, Jaison looked back and Aslam gave him a sly smile.

We reached the tea stall and Jaison asked for two small glasses of tea. Then he pulled my plump cheeks and said, "Why is my Chunnu angry with me?"

I was furious and spoke to him in a low angry voice, "If you don't even know why I'm angry, then there is not much point in talking to you."

Trying to placate me, Jaison said, "What's happened sweetheart? I seriously don't know what's wrong."

By then I was about to blow my top, "Look at your watch and tell me at what time you came to the office today?"

Jaison sounded exasperated, "Oh man, now what's this issue with time? It's a quarter to eleven."

Turning red in the face I said, "You told me in the morning that you would see me at nine thirty in the office today. I'm very punctual and just for you I came early, even before nine thirty but you didn't even reach office by ten!"

Jaison hit his forehead with his left palm and said, "Oh man, how could I forget? I'm such a fool…. I..I..I'm really sorry, darling."

But I was in no mood to forgive. I said, "No, don't say sorry. All you boys are the same. You'll never understand that time is precious. I was waiting like a mad girl in the office just because you asked me to come at nine thirty. I wanted you to be the first to have the gujiyas I brought from home before anyone else. So much so, I didn't even open my sweet box because of you."

Jaison gave me a flying kiss and apologised. Playfully, he held his own ears, so as to say, "I'll never do it again."

I relented, "It's ok for now but next time, please don't make me wait for so long."

We finished our tea and came back to the office. We entered the office together and saw that our boss was sitting on his chair. We started walking apart trying to show him that we were just colleagues. But it seemed that the boss had smelt that there was something between the two of us.

We took our seats. I unlocked my system and started discussing the design of the web portal with the other trainees. At the same time, I opened Google to search for some tutorials. Alongside, I started doing my coding also. Suddenly a message flashed on my screen, "Hey hardworking lady! You'll go a long way in life. I'm sure about it."

I replied to Jaison, "Thanks. Your confidence makes me feel better! In life, I have so many dreams. I want to be successful."

Another message from Jaison, "Hey, where are those snacks? I'm feeling hungry."

I replied, "Wait. Let the boss go out for lunch. Then we'll eat."

After two hours, the boss went out for lunch. I opened my bag and took out two jars full of gujiyas. I called everyone to taste them. Everyone gathered around me and ate one or two pieces. All of them enjoyed eating the gujiyas my mother had so lovingly made for me.

Jaison ate one gujiya after another. Half a jar was still full of gujiyas. Each gujiya was filled with sweet mawa. Normally one cannot eat more than two at a time as they are very heavy. I looked at Jaison munching away and asked him to stop eating. "Hey stop, you've already eaten ten. Please don't eat too many. They'll cause you indigestion and you'll feel sick."

Jaison said, "Oh, I love eating sweets and don't you worry. Nothing will happen to me. You know that I am fond of eating and I can eat quite a lot!

We both laughed together while talking about his huge appetite. After about half an hour, Jaison clutched his stomach tightly and said, "Oh man, I have to run to the loo!

I laughed, "I told you not to eat too much and now see what's happened."

Jaison said, "This is how it normally happens with me." He rushed to the restroom and closed the door with a bang. Aslam looked at me and laughed. After a few minutes, Jaison shouted from inside, "Hey Aslam, there's no water in the toilet. Please do something!"

It was so funny that all of us burst out laughing. Aslam ran downstairs to get some water from a restaurant. The owner of the restaurant told Aslam that as it was summer, the water supply was very poor. Aslam requested him for a bottle of water. The restaurant owner gave him a chilled bottle of water from his refrigerator. Aslam came back running and knocked on the door of the rest room. Jaison opened the door a little and took the bottle. After a few minutes, he shouted again at Aslam, "You …….. why is the water so cold? I'm freezing." We couldn't control ourselves and laughed nonstop. After some time, Jaison emerged from the rest room and informed every one with a straight face not to use the toilet because there was no water.

Our boss came in after lunch time was over. Everyone got back to their work. In the evening, a message flashed on my screen, "Hey, in the next half an hour will you come out with me to Sukhna Lake? I want to spend some quality time with you."

I replied, "Ok, but in office only Aslam knows about us and others are just suspicious about our relationship. If we will leave together then everyone will come to know about us."

Jaison sent another message, "Don't worry, you leave at the usual time and I'll leave after half an hour."

When it was half past six, I got up from my seat and asked the boss, "Sir, may I leave early today? I came back early in the morning from my hometown so I'm feeling tired. I have completed coding of some portion of the portal also." He agreed and I left for the day.

I went back to the PG, took a shower, dressed in a pink salwar kameez and sprayed a lot of deodorant that had a floral perfume. I was ready for my first date.

After forty five minutes Jaison called me and said, "Hey come to the road that is behind your PG, I'm waiting for you." I told Harpreet Aunty that I was going out with my school friends and would not be eating dinner that night.

I was so excited. I rushed to meet Jaison. He was waiting for me under a tree. When he saw me he asked me to hold him and ride pillion on his scooter. I held him by the waist. That was the first time I felt so close to him. I liked the cologne he had used and told him so. In his inimitable style, Jaison took a deep breath and said, "Hmm, you smell divine!"

We reached Sukhna Lake. Jaison parked his scooter and we both reached the steps around the lake. We sat there and enjoyed a romantic evening together. He looked at me and said, "My Chunnu's looking so beautiful today. You're a typical Indian beauty. I like you best in salwar kameez, rather than in western outfits. You don't know how beautiful you are. Look at yourself through my eyes." I smiled and my cheeks turned red.

We held hands and sat close, gazing at each other's eyes for a long time. I felt very happy, mesmerised by our closeness. The lake, surrounded by hills, seemed full of dim red lights. The orange setting sun, the lake and the hills were enough to make that evening magical. A few couples were enjoying their evening together in boats in the middle of the lake.

Suddenly, we were rudely jolted out of our reverie. A police woman came and shouted at us, "Hey, don't sit so close to the water. Leave this place at once."

I asked, "Why is she screaming like this?" Jaison said, "She's doing it for our safety, so that we don't fall into the lake by any chance."

We decided it was best to leave that place. It was eight o'clock and I was feeling hungry. We ate gol gappas and chana bhatura at a stall near the lake. Jaison took me to a famous restaurant in sector 35 and both of us ordered spicy tandoori chicken there.

I looked at my wrist watch and shouted at Jaison, "It's nine o'clock. Hey, come on, wind up fast and take me to my PG otherwise Aunty won't allow me to enter the flat if I get late by another half hour. We ate quickly and Jaison drove me back to my PG.

The following day when he came to the office, I was sitting with one of my male colleagues discussing the technical design of our portal. The whole day that boy sat close to me and we worked on the same computer. I was so busy that I wasn't even able to look at Jaison or exchange any glances with him. I didn't even go out with Aslam and Jaison for our evening ritual of tea and snacks. That day was the deadline for finishing the technical design of our web portal. So we were worked at breakneck speed to meet the deadline. I left office at nine thirty that day and Jaison dropped me home.

After dinner I got a call from him. He was sounding very low on the phone. I asked him why he was sounding so sad. He didn't reply, but in a small voice said, "It's just that I'm not feeling well. I saw the welcome page of the web portal that you guys designed. It's looking good. You guys worked very hard. The whole day the two of you were working on the same computer."

I understood immediately and said, "Oh! So that is the problem. Don't act smart Jaison and talk to me openly. I know why you're so upset but I want to hear it from you, otherwise there's no point of this relationship." I got angry with him and disconnected the phone. Both of us had huge egos so we didn't try to call each other back. I wasn't able to sleep. I kept tossing and turning in bed while my roommate was busy on the phone with her boyfriend. At around half past midnight, my phone rang again.

I picked up the phone but I didn't talk. From the other side Jaison said, "Why aren't you talking to me now. Don't be so complex. Your silence kills me, honestly. Ok, if you want to hear the truth then listen. I was feeling jealous when you were sitting close to your colleague. I know both of you were working together and there is no point feeling jealous. But at that time, watching the two of you together, I couldn't think straight. I felt very possessive about you. I'm sorry Chunnu."

My heart melted and I forgave him that very instant, "You are my Nariyal and I do love you very much. Don't ever feel like that in your life for I'm committed to you. But you'll have to understand that in future I may have many male colleagues at work." ."

I felt Jaison accepted my explanation for he said, "You're my Chunnu and I know my sweetheart is very hardworking. You don't worry, I'll always be there to support you in your career and I'll never be an obstacle in your career path. It was just a for moment and in future, I'll try not to behave this way."

I said, "Thanks, jaan. You're my love. I love you so much. Next time I'll try my best not to hurt you in any way."

Jaison and I used to talk to each other a lot. Every day our call would start at eleven thirty at night and end at two o'clock. With time, our relationship reached a point where I used to talk, walk, eat and do everything using a hands free phone while talking to Jaison.

One day, Jaison's mother caught him red handed while he was talking to me on the phone. She asked him, "Who do you talk to these days? You don't even sleep at night but you keep talking. What's the matter?"

Being very dominating and assertive by nature, Jaison wasn't afraid of anyone in his family. He told his mother directly, "Mom, I'm in love with a girl."

His mother was a very simple lady and good at heart but she was worried about their reputation in society. She asked him, "Who is she and what does she do?"

I was listening to everything on the phone. Jaison replied, "Mom, she's a Hindu girl from Yamuna Nagar, we work in the same office."

Thinking back, I feel at that very moment I must have stopped breathing. I could sense the shock Jaison's mother was feeling. She shouted, "What? What on earth are you talking about Jaison?"

Then she started talking to him in Malayalam. I couldn't understand a single word but I could easily make out that the two of them were arguing.

Meanwhile, Jaison disconnected the phone. My mind was in a whirl and I was under a lot of mental stress wondering what could possibly be taking place between Jaison and his mother. I seemed to have lost my appetite but I didn't want to answer any questions so I quietly went with all the girls to the dining area.

Jaison called me up after sometime. By then I had finished my dinner.

I was relieved to hear him say, "Hi Chunnu."

"What happened? Why did you disconnect the phone?"

Jaison said, "You know my mother and I were fighting because of our relationship."

I couldn't take it any longer, "What did she say?"

"Well, she reacted in a way I had expected her to," Jaison replied. "How could you choose a girl who doesn't belong to our religion? You'll let me down in church and I'll never be respected in society. What will I tell all my relatives? This relationship will never be accepted by any of our relatives or church members."

She wants her daughter-in-law to be a typical Keralite, Christian, Malayalee girl. She cannot accept any girl into the family who is not from her culture or her religion.

I panicked, "Oh my God! If this is the war going on at your end then what will happen when my family comes to know about this relationship?"

Jaison said, "My mother is crying bitterly because I shouted at her. I've said sorry to her for hurting her sentiments. But I also told her that you are my life and I cannot live without you."

At that moment I said what I thought was the right thing to do, "Please give the phone to your mother. I want to talk to her."

Now it was Jaison's turn to panic, "What?"

But I was sure of what I was doing, "Yes, I will also say sorry to her."

He said, "Ok" and gave the phone to his mother.

I said calmly, "Hi Aunty, I'm Naina. Jaison has probably told you about me. How are you?"

She did not reply.

I said, "Aunty, I know what has taken place between you and Jaison and I'm sorry about that. It's happened because of me. But please don't cry." There was complete silence from the other end.

After that, she gave the phone back to Jaison.

He asked, "Hi, are you there?" I replied, "Yes, I'm listening to you."

Jaison said, "You don't worry. We'll have to face it. I've told my mother clearly that I love you a lot. I have my way in my family and I don't listen to anyone so no one can stop me from loving you. All said and done, she's my mother and she loves me a lot. She'll definitely understand my feelings for you and she'll accept you. You go to sleep now and we'll talk tomorrow. Bye, love you sweetheart."

Our late night phone conversations continued this way. Jaison's mother also stopped telling him that our relationship was not right. She would talk to me once in a while just to say 'hello'. A part of her accepted me but she was scared of her relatives and society.

Jaison and I started spending our weekends together and now I went home only once every month. Whenever my parents asked me why I didn't go home more often, I always gave lame excuses of there being a lot of work in the office.

Every weekend was so special and romantic for me. One Friday, I called up Jaison in the evening to make plans for the weekend. "Hi my Nariyal, what are you doing? Have you eaten your dinner?"

"Yes darling, I am done with my dinner."

I teased him, "You fatty, I'm sure you'll eat again in the middle of night," and I laughed.

Jaison replied, "Just you wait my Chunnu and I'll eat you too. Because my Chunnu, you're soooo cute. I want to eat your chubby cheeks and your little, little nose. May I?"

I smiled to myself and felt a little shy. Hurriedly I said, "Leave all this. Let's come to the point. What is your plan for tomorrow?"

Jaison said, "Tomorrow we'll go to 'Fun Republic' at around eleven thirty and then in the evening we will go to the park in sector 45. I want to spend the whole day with you."

I said, "Ok, my Nariyal. I feel so happy and safe whenever you're around me or with me. I love you a lot."

The following day when I got up, I smiled at the rising sun from my balcony. I was happy as I was going to spend the whole day with my love. I had my morning tea and breakfast. Then I opened my cupboard and started inspecting it from top to bottom. Unlike Jaison, I'm a much organised person. I love to keep things in an organised manner so that it's easy for me to find what I'm looking for in just a few minutes.

Jaison always keeps his wardrobe in a huge mess. Each time, before going to office, he has to empty out his wardrobe in order to select his formal clothes.

I wondered aloud, "What should I wear today? I looked through my clothes and settled on a sleeveless pink top, red scarf and blue jeans. Everyone had always told me that I looked beautiful in my pink top. My mother used to say that pink suited my complexion and enhanced my looks.

I bathed and took special care to get ready. Once on the road, I covered my face with my scarf. I never forgot to cover my face while going out with Jaison so that no one would recognise me. Chandigarh wasn't far from Yamuna Nagar and I always lived in the fear that someone known to the family would see me with Jaison on his scooter. Jaison picked me up from the same place. We reached 'Fun Republic' and booked tickets for a Hindi movie. After watching the movie, we decided to order Chinese food which turned out to be really good.

In the evening, we went to the park in sector 45 and sat close together on a bench. Jaison held my hand and said, "Naina, even when I'm old I want to come and sit with you in a park. I will love you even when you lose all your teeth and have a wrinkled face. I want to enjoy samosas and evening tea with you in our balcony. Do you feel the same way about me?"

My eyes filled with tears. I had never dreamt that some boy could actually love me this way. I was touched that he was not just attracted to me physically. I said, "I have always wanted a man like you Jaison. Someone who can respect his woman, love her and support her. I would want to get married to you. I know this journey will be difficult for us but we will fight it out. Jaison gently wiped the tears rolling down my cheeks.

Suddenly we saw a couple sitting on a bench in a corner far from us. The sun had set and it was getting dark. Nothing was clearly visible but we could see that the couple was kissing passionately. I looked at Jaison and asked him, "What are they doing? This is a public place and the police may catch them red handed."

Jaison was his usual nonchalant self. "Nothing happens. Many times I have seen couples hiding in corners or kissing under a tree. Poor things! They need some privacy somewhere to express their love."

We looked at each other and I suddenly asked him a question, "Have you ever kissed a girl?" Jaison replied, "No, I don't even know how to kiss. But we can try if you like…."

I smiled and patted his cheeks .I said, "No, no! And I mean a big NO. Come on, let's go now. It's getting dark."

Jaison started his scooter but looked dismayed. "Oh man, it has very little petrol but I think I will be able to drop you to your PG."

I felt very irritated at his carelessness. I lost my temper, "Why are you so careless? We were out for the whole day and you could have got your tank filled any time but now, just when I have to reach back on time, you start wondering whether we'll be able to make it to my PG. When will you bring some discipline in your life?"

Jaison replied, "Please don't start all over again and cool down please. I'll get it filled from some petrol pump nearby." For a few kilometres we didn't find any petrol pump and finally when we were about to give up, we saw one. We were about five minutes away from the pump, when the scooter stopped in the middle of the road.

I started off again, "Now look at your foolishness. I really don't know what will happen today. If I reach late, then Aunty will shout at me and maybe she will not allow me to enter the PG. All this is happening only because of you."

It was nearly nine o'clock and there was hardly any traffic on the roads. Jaison said, "Please be patient, the petrol pump is nearby. We'll push the scooter to the petrol pump. It took us twenty minutes before we could reach the petrol pump. We got the scooter re-fuelled and then Jaison finally dropped me at the PG. It was almost thirty five minutes after nine.

I thanked God.

These happy romantic days went on for a few months. During this period, I was also struggling for a job. My training was nearing completion. One day Jaison saw me looking depressed in the office. He suggested, "Let's go out for a coffee."

Aslam, Jaison and I went to a restaurant to have coffee. Jaison asked me, "What's happened Chunnu? Why are you so upset?"

I told him, "My training period is nearing completion. My parents have already spent a lot of money on my training and I still don't have any job in hand. You know I am career oriented. I know I've done my post-graduation from a small private institute so I'll have to struggle to get a job. It won't be easy for me to enter a big IT company. I don't know if I can land a job in Chandigarh itself. I also don't want to go far away from you."

Aslam consoled me, "Why do you worry so much? We all know you are very talented and hardworking and you'll definitely get a job."

Jaison said, "Don't worry Chunnu, you start looking for a job and I'll take you to different companies for interviews."

We finished our coffee and got back to our work. I uploaded my resume on a few job portals. In the first month I hardly got two or three calls. Jaison groomed me for the introductory rounds of interviews while I prepared for the technical rounds. He took me to all the three companies - one was a BPO, one had only fifteen employees and the third one had only three employees. I declined the BPO offer and tried my luck in the other two companies. Nothing came off it as they were looking for experienced persons while I was a fresher.

I was very upset and kept talking to my parents about this situation. My parents were very supportive. After some time, I finished both my training and my post-graduation. I continued to stay in Chandigarh. Jaison supported me during this period of struggle. After a few months, I got a job offer from the same company in which I had completed my training. My boss offered me a job based on my performance. My parents were happy when I told them.

I wanted to meet my aunt in Delhi who had supported me during my college days. I asked my boss for permission to join after three days as I wanted to go to Delhi and meet my aunt and he agreed.

Jaison dropped me to the bus stand. I bought a ticket for Delhi and boarded the bus. We looked at each other through the bus window. We were both preoccupied with our thoughts as we said good bye to each other. Neither of us knew what to expect next.

After five and half hours, I got down at Delhi's Indira Gandhi bus stand and caught another bus for R.K. Puram. I reached my aunt's place and gave her a surprise. Both uncle and aunty were very happy when I broke the news of my job offer.

I was not attending to any calls on my cell phone as I did not want to pay the extra roaming charges. I didn't know why one of my friends was trying to reach me. I found that there were twenty missed calls on my cell phone. In the evening, I got a message from Jaison. "I logged into your system at office and found that one of your friends had left a message on instant messenger. There is a walk-in interview tomorrow in Gurgaon in one of the top five Indian IT companies." I was also surprised to see a message on my phone from one of my friends. It said "Call me, it's urgent."

My mind was in a whirl. I didn't know what destiny had in store for me. Had I come to Delhi for a reason? I called my friend Rosa who had sent me the text message. Rosa screamed at me, "You so and so! Why didn't you receive my call? I tried to call you twenty times. Anyway, now listen to me carefully. We have a walk-in interview in Gurgaon, the day after tomorrow. Our whole class is going there."

I felt frantic, "Oh God, I had come to Delhi to relax. I don't even have books to prepare for an interview. What will I do now? I don't know what I will say in the interview."

Rosa said, "Don't worry. I am in Gurgaon, staying at Nafisa's place. We have many books here. That will be sufficient for the three of us to prepare for an interview in just one day. Why don't you join us tomorrow?"

I said, "Ok, just text me your address."

I got the address the next minute. I told my aunt everything. Uncle told me that I could get a direct bus to Gurgaon from sector 1 R.K. Puram.

I informed my parents about the developments, packed my stuff and next morning, I reached Gurgaon bus stop. I was visiting this city for the very first time. The bus stop was in old Gurgaon. I found old Gurgaon to be completely different from Chandigarh. It was dusty and congested with heaps of garbage lying everywhere. People had small houses in congested colonies and I could see cows sitting on roads. I could not understand how IT companies could be set up at such a place. I felt peeved and I was not able to digest the fact that after Chandigarh, life could bring me to such a place. At Yamuna Nagar, I had always heard that Gurgaon was like mini Singapore. Now I simply couldn't believe my eyes.

I was already missing Chandigarh and Jaison a lot. But I had to move ahead and ignore my feelings. Following my friend's directions,

I reached sector 14 and searched for my friend's house. All my friends were meeting after such a long time. Nafisa had completed her training in one of the IT companies in Gurgaon. Her brother was working there and with his referral, it was possible for her to get her training there.

Disgustedly, I asked Nafisa, '"Hey, how can you stay in such a city? I am coming from Chandigarh which is such a clean and planned city."

Nafisa said, "Darling you're new to this city and you have seen only old Gurgaon. When you see new Gurgaon, you will understand the actual lifestyle of people here. There are so many IT companies here and people are earning so much. Many people like us who come from small towns have made their lives in this city. You just relax and we'll have lunch together. After that, we will prepare for the interview."

I called up Jaison, "Hi darling, I'm missing you and Chandigarh so much. I don't know what I will do in the interview. We have just one day left and we need to go through all the books of our six semesters to get through the interview. It's such a big company and I'm sure I won't be able to clear the interview. It will be tough."

Jaison consoled me, "You don't worry. I have a strong intuition that you'll be selected. You are very hardworking. You just start preparing for the interview. Bye and best of luck."

After lunch, my friends and I studied continuously till late in the night praying all the while that our interview would go off well.

Next morning, I dressed up smartly in salwar kameez. I hired an auto rickshaw from sector 14 to Kapashera - the border of Delhi and Gurgaon - in Udyog Vihar. For the first time in my life, I saw so many people on the road. It seemed as if it was only meant for people to walk and that no trucks and cars were allowed on that road. It was really difficult for anyone to drive there. Not only this, I also saw an open drainage system on both sides of the road. This was probably the worst place in the whole of Gurgaon. There were several manufacturing companies at that place which provided employment to many villagers. Udyog Vihar is the industrial area in Gurgaon. I felt uncomfortable and frightened in this strange place. I really missed the familiar surroundings of Chandigarh and my love, Jaison. It was difficult for girls to walk in that crowd, so to reach the office, we had to hire a rickshaw from Kapashera though it was just at a distance of five minutes. On reaching that place, I saw that many of my classmates were standing outside the gate. I felt happy meeting my friends after a long time. Like me, everyone was struggling to get a decent job. There were approximately twenty people from my class who had come to attend the walk-in interview. The security guard asked everyone to make their entries in the register and take a visitor's card.

All of us were asked to wait at the reception. I entered the building and for the first time in my life, I understood what a reputed IT company looks like. The building was very well done up from inside. A black leather sofa was placed in one corner of the reception area. There was a coffee machine and a water dispenser in the other corner. The reception area was big enough to accommodate fifty people. There was a big glass frame on the front wall which had all kinds of achievement awards placed in it. The receptionist was a beautiful lady dressed smartly in a red saree. She took everyone's resume and informed the HR department on phone about the candidates. A lot of glass, wood and steel had been used in the construction of the work place and the building was centrally air conditioned. It was relaxing to be in the air conditioned comfort inside; outside, it was too hot. Some people enjoyed tea, coffee or tomato soup from the dispensing machine while the others were busy revising. I felt relaxed. From childhood I had the habit of not revising anything before an exam. I just remained calm and enjoyed the ambience. I left everything to my destiny and was ready to face my interview with confidence. I did not worry about my selection and deliberately kept my mind blank. After an hour, the receptionist asked everyone to go to the canteen on the third floor.

One of the administrative staff members escorted us to the canteen. The canteen was so spacious it could have easily accommodated three thousand people at a time. In one corner there was fast food, tea and juice available throughout office hours. There were many smartly designed black chairs and glass tables all over the canteen. Three members of the HR department were sitting together. Trying to create a friendly environment, they welcomed all of us and asked us to relax. After some time, they asked each one of us to introduce ourselves by turn. This was the test of our communication skills and confidence.

As usual, most of the candidates did not have even average communication skills, so some introductions were hilarious but somehow, no one laughed.

Then it was my turn. I knew how to introduce myself as I had read about it many times on the internet. I talked about myself. One of the HR team members asked me, "To be a part of any organisation, which qualities, according to you, are the most important?"

I answered without hesitation, "For me, loyalty and honesty are the two most important qualities."

Then I was asked to tell them about my hobbies. I replied confidently that my favourite hobbies were dancing, singing and cooking.

I was taken aback when the HR person asked me to sing a song in front of twenty five people. I realised he was testing my confidence. I sang a song from the Hindi movie Sarfarosh. I have always been a good singer right from my college days. This time also, I sang it well. Everyone clapped and my introductory round came to an end.

After completing the introductory round, the HR team selected fifteen people out of twenty five. I was one of the fifteen.

The next round was the aptitude test. We were given seventy five objective questions and we were supposed to solve it in one hour.

After we completed this round, we were asked to wait at the reception for the results. After twenty five minutes, one of the HR persons came with a list in his hand and announced the names of ten people. I was happy to see that I had cleared the second round also.

The following day we were called for the technical round. I reached there, dressed in a black salwar kameez, with my certificates and a copy of my resume.

At the reception I met many freshers but most of them were not from my college. One of my classmates and I were lucky to have cleared the first two rounds. I met a girl called Manisha from Yamuna Nagar. We were meeting for the first time. Yamuna Nagar is a small town and while talking to each other, we discovered that we had a common friend whose brother was my brother Priyanshu's best friend. It was indeed a small world!

I felt comfortable that I had found someone from my home town. We started planning that if we both were finally selected in this company, then we would stay together in a PG accommodation as it would be easy for us to adjust with each other's lifestyle because we belonged to the same town.

After two hours, I was called to a small glass meeting room for the technical round. There was a big black table and I was escorted to one end of the table. Two persons were sitting at the other end. It was a peaceful room. Somehow, the silence in the room made me feel more confident. Only one person was firing questions one after another and I soon realised that not all the questions were technical. A few of the questions were very sharp – "If you are a senior person in your team and you have to deal with a junior whose attitude is not good then how will you handle this situation?"

I answered, "I will first have a one on one session with the person to make him understand that he should improve his attitude. I will also give him some time to show me that. But after that time period if there is no improvement, then I will bring it to the notice of my senior managers."

And then there were many questions from physics and chemistry also. I noticed that the other person in the room was not speaking but only observing me. I had read about observation on the internet so I knew how to conduct myself.

My technical round lasted for twenty to thirty minutes. When I came out of the meeting room, I was asked to wait outside. The other candidates who were waiting there surrounded me and asked me what questions I had been asked and how the interview had gone. I told them what had transpired.

After one more hour, I was called for the final round. The HR person asked me a few questions and asked me to leave for the day. He also told me that if selected, I would receive a call within the next week.

It was almost six thirty and I was new to this city. I was missing Jaison also. Instead of going back to my aunt in Delhi, my classmate (who was from Ambala city) and I hired an auto rickshaw to Gurgaon bus stand and caught a direct bus to Chandigarh.

There was a huge traffic jam in Delhi and it took us almost seven hours to reach Chandigarh. We reached Chandigarh only in the morning. Somehow I had a strong intuition that I would be staying in Chandigarh only for a few more days.

I reached office at nine thirty, eager to meet Jaison. As usual, he came in late, only by a quarter to eleven. He was excited to see me but never expressed his feelings for me in front of anyone except Aslam.

At lunch time, Jaison asked me to eat lunch with him in the restaurant below the office.

We ordered chana bhatura and tea. After placing the order, he looked at me lovingly and held my hand. He said only one thing, "I missed you a lot. I don't know why but I get this feeling that you'll go away from me. I know you'll get selected in that company and leave this city for good."

I replied with tears in my eyes, "I missed you too. Now I cannot think of my life without you. You have filled my life with lots of love and happiness."

Jaison wiped my tears. After lunch, while sipping tea he asked me, "So how was your interview?" I narrated everything to him.

He told me, "We're meeting after so many days, let's go out for dinner today."

We spent the evening together and had a candle lit romantic dinner.

After a few days, I got a call when I was in office, "Hi, am I talking to Naina?"

I asked, "Yes, who's this?"

"Hi Naina, this is Mithlesh." He was from the HR department of the IT company in Gurgaon."

"Hi Mithlesh, how are you?"

"I am fine, thanks. I want to congratulate you on being selected in our company."

I could not believe my ears! I was going to start my career in one of the top five Indian IT companies. He asked me to join after five days.

I called up my parents and shared this piece of good news with them. The same day I also got to know from my parents that my brother had been selected by one of the top steel companies of India. It was a moment of double celebration for everyone in our family. I was surprised to know that my brother and I were going to join two different companies on the same day and that too, in the same city!

My parents were filled with joy and their happiness knew no bounds. Their struggles had borne fruit and their dreams had come true. Both their children had got settled in a big city and in big companies. I called up Priyanshu and congratulated him.

Suddenly Jaison came into the office. I looked at him and realised that it was time to go away from him. I could not bear the pain and left my seat without looking at him.

When half an hour had passed and I hadn't come back to my seat, Jaison went out in search of me. He found me at the back of the office building. I was standing in one corner of the balcony facing the road.

He called out to me but I didn't reply. He then asked me to turn around. I turned around and hugged him. I was crying bitterly. He hugged me tight and begged me not to cry.

I sobbed uncontrollably. Jaison asked me, "What's happened to you and why are you crying?"

I said, "Now I'll have to go away from you. Jaison, you know I've always waited for this good thing to happen in my life, but now that I've got it, I'm not happy as I don't want to go away from you. I have seen you almost every day in these last eight months and suddenly my destiny is taking me away from you. What is all this? I can't think of my life without you. I can't live without you. We have spent so many weekends and evenings together. I've laughed with you and I've cried with you. We've spent beautiful moments together and now suddenly, everything will disappear from our life. I cannot accept this big change."

Jaison consoled me and congratulated me by turn. He said, "I knew you're so hardworking and ambitious, you'd definitely get selected. See, it just happened. This is a small company. God has shown you the path to start your career in a big IT company. You're the lucky one who got this chance just after a struggle of eight months and even though you had passed out from a private institute. Think of your classmates who may have to struggle for more than a year to get such a decent job. Do not lose this opportunity and just go. God is taking our test to see if we can continue to love each other even when we're separated. You've made a permanent place in my heart and now no one can replace you. We'll get married and my love for you will never get diminished. You'll have to do it for the sake of your career. I'll always come to meet you once a month and I'll talk to you every day on the phone. Why do you worry so much?"

Days passed quickly. I gave notice to Harpreet Aunty that I would be leaving in the next five days as I had got a job in Gurgaon.

Jaison asked me, "Have you found PG accommodation in Gurgaon?"

I said, "No, not yet, but I know some of my seniors from college who are staying in Gurgaon. I'll contact them and I'll definitely get a PG there. Until I get a PG, I'll stay with my aunt."

Jaison said, "Ok, I'll come along with you when you go to Delhi. You will have a lot of luggage."

I smiled, "Ok, that'll be good. I have spoken to my aunt. She won't be at her place at that time, she'll leave the keys with her neighbours. So there should be no problem. You can drop me at my aunt's place and no one needs to know about it."

Only three days were left. I started packing my belongings.

My father called me and asked, "How will you go to Delhi all by yourself with so many luggages? I will come to Chandigarh and we'll go to Delhi together."

I said, "No Papa, please don't worry. I don't have that much stuff. I'll manage."

He insisted, "I know my daughter has grown up now but I am still your father and I worry a lot about you so I will come."

I was frantic, "No Papa, I'm telling you. It will be so hectic for you. First you'll come to Chandigarh and then you'll carry my luggage from Chandigarh to Delhi. Don't worry, I'll manage."

I'd already planned this journey with Jaison, so I had to convince my father not to travel with me. I planned to leave for Delhi with him early Sunday morning and reach there by afternoon. I told Jaison my plan.

All too soon it was Sunday. Jaison's mother knew that he was going to drop me. And being a good hearted lady, she packed lunch for both of us.

Jaison came in an auto rickshaw to my PG and picked up my luggage. We reached the bus stand and got two tickets for the air conditioned Volvo bus.

For the first time in my life, I was going to travel in an AC bus. I thanked Jaison for giving me this happiness. He told me that he didn't want me to go in a crowded bus so for my comfort, he had bought tickets of an air conditioned bus. He said, "I'm earning so I can give you this comfort." We got the corner seats and the bus departed for Delhi.

I said, "Jaison, I don't know what is next in our lives but it will be very tough for me to accept that I will not see you every day in Gurgaon. Now we can only talk on the phone. Also, my brother will be living in the same city, so we'll have to be very careful while meeting once a month. My parents wanted me to stay with my brother but I told them that living in an independent house would be very expensive, so we should stay in separate PGs. I did this for us. If I stay with him then it'll be impossible for us to meet."

I kept on holding his hand and put my head on his shoulder and slept. In the afternoon when we felt hungry, Jaison took out two big lunch boxes. They were wrapped in newspaper. I unwrapped the boxes and we started eating. After lunch, my eye suddenly fell on an advertisement in that newspaper. It was for a job in a call centre in Gurgaon.

I said excitedly, "Look at this, Jaison. God's with us. There's a job opening in Gurgaon. You can attend the interview – it's on next Saturday. It'll give us a chance to stay close to each other in Gurgaon. That way, we'll be able to meet every day."

Jaison said, "But Chunnu, it's a call centre job. I don't want to spoil my life by just being on phone all through the night."

I reasoned with him, "Jaison, it'll give us a chance to stay close. Also, you're doing your MBA through correspondence and want to make your career in sales and marketing. This way, by joining the call centre you might get to know something about it."

Jaison said, "Ok fine, I'll give it a try for the sake of our love."

In five and a half hours, Jaison and I reached New Delhi ISBT. We hired a prepaid auto rickshaw from there to R.K. Puram. It took one hour for us to reach my aunt's place. I didn't take him inside my aunt's house as I was afraid of my aunt's neighbours. I was scared that if by any chance they saw me with Jaison, they would tell tales to my aunt which would make it difficult for me.

Several questions were going on in my mind at that moment. Was I meeting Jaison for the last time? Would he get a job in Gurgaon? Would we ever stay close together again?

I gave him a kiss and said goodbye to him with a heavy heart. Jaison returned to the Inter State Bus Terminus in the same auto rickshaw. I cried a lot and Jaison kept looking at me from the rear window of the auto rickshaw until I was out of sight.

I consoled myself, "Don't cry Naina. We will meet again," and I wiped my tears. I took the house keys from my aunt's neighbours and entered her house.

5

Life in Gurgaon

I settled down at a paying guest accommodation in Gurgaon with Manisha and another of my classmates. All of us had been selected by the same company and given job offers. We shared a room big enough to accommodate three people. Each one's share came to three thousand five hundred rupees per month. This was an up gradation from Harpreet Aunty's PG in Chandigarh – now we had a room cooler for summers and hot water in the bathroom during winters, a power backup system, a full time servant for cooking, cleaning and washing, we could use an iron in our room and we were given three meals a day.

On the first of the month, we reached our office at Kapashera border. The location was disappointing but we were excited because it was our first day. We reported to someone in the administration department. He gave us a four page agreement and asked us to read it carefully and submit it within a week's time after signing it. The agreement had certain terms and conditions and we needed to get it signed by our parents. According to the agreement, if we did not perform well in the tests we could be terminated from the company but if our performance was good, our jobs would be confirmed with the condition of a one and a half year bond with the company. After we were given the agreement, we were asked to complete our fourteen day technical training.

Next day, we met the other twenty five trainees who had joined with us. All of them were fresh post graduates who had come from different places and in a few days we became good friends. I worked hard and performed very well during the training period.

Jaison and I kept in touch on phone. He cleared the call centre interview and was asked to join after one month. My brother found his own PG accommodation which he shared with a couple of boys. Though I was happy and excited that I would once again be meeting Jaison after our one month separation, I was also scared because my brother was staying in the same city. If by any chance he saw us together, all hell would break loose and it would be like a tsunami hitting my family.

One week had passed and on the first weekend, I asked my PG aunty - the lady who had rented out her flat to us - which was the best place in Gurgaon where I could go shopping. Aunty recommended the shopping malls for which Gurgaon is famous.

Manisha, my classmate Divya and I dressed in salwar kameez outfits, wore a little makeup and hired an auto rickshaw from sector 22 to Sadar Bazaar. The driver charged us five rupees each. From Sadar Bazaar we caught a local bus to a shopping mall. The bus was jam-packed and the crowd was really pathetic. It was hard to believe that I was in a big city. I had heard a lot of good things about Gurgaon but that crowd truly left a bad impression on me.

Till now, I had seen only one face of this city, the other side was yet to be explored. We crossed Bata Chowk and Iffco Chowk and from there we reached Metropolitan Mall. I held my breath - for the first time in my life I saw another face of this city - tall, new, shiny, beautiful buildings, glitzy malls and expensive cars – Toyota Camrys, BMWs, Mercedes, Audis among others. There were luxury apartments on either side of the main road and I estimated that their value would be in crores of rupees. I saw young people outside the mall. Everyone was dressed in western attire. People were speaking in English with each other and those coming out of the malls were carrying shopping bags and I recognised many of the brand names. I realised that I was actually in a big city.

Many digital advertisements were flashing on billboards outside the malls. It seemed to be a fantasy world to me as I had never seen anything like this in Yamuna Nagar. There I had always seen ladies of my mother's age dressed either in sarees or salwar kameez but here every woman was dressed either in skirts, dresses, jeans or even in shorts. At the entrance of the mall there was McDonald's. We ordered vegetable burgers with french fries. I loved every bite of it. I loved just sitting there, observing families coming in, eating and moving out. It was far removed from any experience I'd had in Yamuna Nagar.

Then we entered the fully air conditioned mall. There were so many shops there. All of them were selling either big Indian brands or international brands. I feasted my eyes by just looking at the clothes that were displayed at each shop. There were so many good looking western outfits for girls and boys. I'd never worn such clothes in my life.

I saw a white skirt with red flowers printed on it and asked the price. It was for a shocking two thousand rupees. My eyes remained wide open after listening to its price. I turned to my friends and they both said, "My God, it's so expensive! It shouldn't be more than five hundred rupees. And to think, people really come here to shop."

I said, "When I get my first salary then I'll come to this mall to buy these expensive, branded clothes and shoes. I want to live this life."

We floated from shop to shop and did our share of window shopping. We booked tickets for the evening show at PVR cinema at the mall.

We reached the cinema in the evening and when I entered PVR, I was stunned to see the plush red wall to wall carpet there. There were two water dispensers in two corners from where we could help ourselves to chilled water and washrooms for men and women on either side. Just after the entrance there was a big counter from where they sold nachos, popcorn and cold drinks. We bought popcorn and three large cold drinks. It was three times the price at which one could buy from a roadside vendor.

We sank into our comfortable seats and settled down with our popcorn and drinks. I remembered the cinema halls in Yamuna Nagar which were all so smelly. The theatres were old and the interiors had never been maintained. The seats were broken and in such a dilapidated condition that it is difficult to describe it.I, for one, had never been allowed to go to the cinema because my father and my uncles believed that it was not a suitable place for girls since all the boys from the village came to see movies. If there was a scene in the movie where the heroine wore a short dress with a deep neck, people would pass dirty comments, whistle and throw flashlight beams on the actress's body. So families were never comfortable going to cinema halls because a certain section of the audience was sure to misbehave in this manner. I also remember how one day, I went to see a movie in Yamuna Nagar with my school friends without telling my family. But somehow, my uncle came to know about it from somewhere as in a small town, nothing is hidden from any one. After that, a big scene had been created at home.

I remember whenever we wanted to see a good movie, my father would rent a video player at fifty rupees for one night and we would watch many Hindi movies on video tapes.

The PVR experience brought back many Yamuna Nagar memories. In Yamuna Nagar, one could get a movie ticket for twenty five rupees but here in Gurgaon, it would be no exaggeration to say that it was ten times the price. But I still found it worth spending that much extra. The crowd at PVR Gurgaon was decent. After the movie, we went back to our PG.

Soon our training period came to an end. During this time Manisha and I became close friends and I told her about my involvement with Jaison.

After we completed our training, we received confirmation of our jobs. We were asked to submit the agreement to the company within the next three days, after getting it signed by our parents. All of us decided to take leave and go to our hometowns to get the document signed.

Manisha and I left for Yamuna Nagar the same weekend. We caught bus # 797 from Kapashera border to reach the ISBT at New Delhi. From ISBT we caught the bus for Yamuna Nagar. On the way I told Manisha, "I want to tell my family about Jaison. I don't want to keep them in the dark anymore."

While we were on our way home, I got a phone call from Priyanshu. He was happy speaking to me about this and that. He said, "Sis, you've got a good job now so what are your plans for marriage? I'll ask Dad to look for a suitable match for you." Then he laughed, "Or have you found someone?"

I became serious as this was no longer a joke for me. I told him, "Priyanshu, I need to tell you something."

Priyanshu said, "Tell me, what's happened?"

I said, "Actually there is someone in my life."

It was now Priyanshu's turn to become serious and his voice sounded heavy. He asked me, "Who is he and what does he do?"

I said, "Priyanshu, his name is Jaison. He's Christian. We met in Chandigarh. He was working in the same company where I completed my last semester training for my MCA. He's also doing his MBA through correspondence. His parents are from Kerala. His father died two years back. He lives in Chandigarh with his sister and mother."

Priyanshu couldn't contain himself any longer. He shouted at me, "What have you done? You fell in love with someone and that too with a Christian guy? You are a bright girl. How can you think of life with him? I never thought that you would take such a step in life. I'll have to talk to Mom and Dad about this. I won't be able to sleep tonight. You have ruined our reputation and heaped shame on us. We can't tell anyone about this."

I said, "Listen to me Priyanshu, he's actually a very nice guy. It doesn't matter to me in the least if he belongs to some other religion and is struggling at this point in his life.

Priyanshu disconnected the phone. I started crying as I was worried about my visit home. Manisha consoled me, "You are a fighter and a courageous girl. I know you will handle everything well. Don't worry. Only consider how you will convince your family."

After an hour, I got a call from Priyanshu again. He said, "I've told them everything on the phone. They are in shock and all this is just because of you. Mom's blood pressure has shot up. You have to leave this guy even if it's only for their sake. This must end and now! You can only go through an arranged marriage and that too, according to our family's wishes." Saying this he disconnected the phone without caring for my feelings.

On reaching home I rang the doorbell. My hands were trembling and my pulse was racing. I was feeling very anxious. My father opened the door and stared at me. He did not say anything. I entered my bedroom. My mother was sitting there with an ashen face, as if she had lost all her senses. It seemed she would lose her life in a few seconds.

I hugged her. I cried, "Mom what's happened to you? Why aren't you talking to me?"

There was complete silence in the room. My father's voice cut me to the thick. It was strict, cold and distant, "Why did you do such a thing? Surely, you understand that this is not a suitable match for you. We cannot allow you to marry a Christian. We will never be able to show our face to anyone in society. What have you done? Why did I ever send you to Chandigarh all alone? For the first time in your life you stayed away from home and fell in love with such a person?"

My mother asked me to leave him forever and promised to find a suitable match for me.

I could not utter a single word and kept quiet. None of us slept that night. I was in a state of shock. My parents were frantic about me and the whole situation. They asked me to forget this whole episode and move forward in life but according to their wishes.

The following morning, I called up Jaison in Chandigarh and told him everything. I kept on crying for about two hours on the phone. At the end, Jaison asked me, "Now do you want to continue this relationship or not?"

I could not say either a "Yes" or a "No" and was silent for a very long time. My father snatched the phone from my hands and started talking to Jaison, "Hello, I'm Naina's father."

Jaison said, "Hello Sir, how are you?"

My father did not mince words nor was he in a mood to stand on ceremony. He came straight to the point, "I'm not fine and it's all because of you. I'm sure you are a very mature person and can very well understand that this relationship can never turn into marriage. I absolutely will not allow my daughter to go and marry someone out of our religion. What will I say to my relatives? It will be impossible for me to survive in this society. I request you to forget Naina."

As soon as I took the phone back from my father, Jaison started off, "Chunnu, you've become a part of my life andI'll miss you very much. My heart is crying for you but your father has told me his final decision. I will miss you till my last breath. You will always be the love of my life. I hope you get married to a nice man and forget me soon. I've resigned from the company in Chandigarh and will join the call centre in Gurgaon. I cannot leave the Gurgaon job because of this complication and I also have no other option at this moment. I cannot sit at home without a job because I have to send money to my sister. So I'll be in Gurgaon but we will never meet. This is goodbye forever, my sweet Chunnu. I will always love you."

I kept the phone down and started crying loudly. I cried the whole day. The following day my brother also arrived. He started shouting at me. I kept quiet and said nothing to him. I was not in any condition to say anything to anyone. Jaison had just walked away from my life and now life had no meaning for me. Nothing made sense anymore and everything seemed meaningless.

Priyanshu told my parents not to send me back to Gurgaon and to get me married to a suitable guy as soon as possible.

Suddenly I lost control and broke the silence with just one sentence, "If Jaison isn't there in my life, then there isn't place for anyone else in my life."

Priyanshu was livid. He searched my bag and took out the agreement. He said, "I'll burn these papers and you'll never be able to go back to Gurgaon."

My father snatched the papers from his hands, "Have you gone mad? We should behave maturely at this moment. We all know that what Naina has done is wrong. But she is my daughter. I know she will leave this boy for the sake of her parents. We cannot spoil her career because of this incident. She has worked very hard to reach where she is today. We should support her in her career. I will allow her to leave for Gurgaon but only for the sake of her career."

I stared at Priyanshu and asked my father to sign the agreement. Then I took the papers back. The following day, my father dropped Priyanshu and me to the Yamuna Nagar bus stand and we caught the bus for Gurgaon.

Manisha called me and asked me to get one more ticket for her as she wanted to go back with me. I bought a ticket for Manisha and she arrived at the bus stand in the next fifteen minutes and got into the bus. We sat together while Priyanshu sat on the back seat. I told Manisha that Priyanshu would also be travelling back with us.

My eyes were swollen so Manisha understood what I had gone through at home. I was feeling lost and my mind was blank during the entire journey. I wore my dark shades to hide my tears. Manisha insisted that I should eat something but I didn't feel like touching any food and refused to eat anything.

When the bus entered Gurgaon, Priyanshu got down at Iffco Chowk. He instructed me not to call Jaison and then he left.

Tears rolled down my eyes again. Manisha consoled me. We got down at the Gurgaon bus stop. From there, we reached our PG.

The last eight months were playing like a Hindi movie in my mind. I was missing Jaison badly. I called him up to hear his voice.

Jaison started crying on the phone. He shouted at me in frustration, "Why are you calling me when there is nothing between us. You have given me enough pain. I will pass my life without you. Please don't try to come back in my life. And please don't call me." Saying this he hung up.

I kept on crying. Manisha came into the room with dinner for me. She consoled me and hugged me. She said, "Don't cry. Just pray to God. Jaison and you both love each other very much. God will show you the way and you need to be strong to fight such a situation. So eat something and be strong."

I listened to her and ate my dinner and went to bed to take some rest. My eyes were swollen and paining and I had a severe headache. Manisha applied some pain relieving balm on my forehead and I closed my eyes.

After midnight, my phone rang. I wasn't completely asleep, so I picked up my phone to check the number. It was Jaison. I took the call, "Chunnu, I'm sorry. I was in pain and I said so many things to you. I really love you and I am missing you so much. Will you meet me just once when I come to Gurgaon?"

I replied, "Yes, I want to meet you too but my brother will be keeping an eye at me."

Jaison said, "Ok, in that case, we won't meet. I don't want you to suffer because of me."

While I was talking to Jaison, I saw that our residence phone number was flashing on my phone screen. My father was trying to call me. I asked Jaison to disconnect immediately because if my phone was busy for another few minutes, then my parents would suspect that I was talking to Jaison.

He disconnected quickly and I received a call from home. It was my father, "Hello Naina, please don't break our trust this time. I hope you will not meet that guy again. I want you to come out of all this as soon as possible, then we will look for a suitable match for you."

I screamed at my father and said, "Please stop pressurising me. I've already told you if Jaison is not there in my life then there won't be anyone else. You asked me to leave him. I left him for you but now don't expect anything else from me. My heart will not allow me to marry someone else. Don't try to call me again. Don't think of me as your daughter. From now onwards, I won't come to Yamuna Nagar. I won't talk to you, mom or Priyanshu. You didn't understand my feelings and forced me to kill my feelings for Jaison. You've wronged me. God and I will never forgive you."

My father said, "My dear, please don't cry. We know you're in pain but we can't allow you to carry on with this relationship. You are not in a good frame of mind at this moment, so you're talking to us like this. You are and you always will be our daughter. How can you stop talking to us? It's unthinkable. Please take care of yourself and don't cry."

My father disconnected the phone.

The following morning I was not able to get up. My head hurt very badly and I felt stressed. But Manisha insisted that I should get ready and go to office. She said, "Come to office. It'll be a change for you. It'll take your mind off all this, at least for a while."

We got ready for office and reached at half past eight. I submitted my agreement papers to the 'admin' department and went to the training room. All my batch mates were playing 'antakshri' and enjoying their free time. I was distracted and forgot my pain when they were around me. I was trying to hide my tears and my worries behind my laughter.

After lunch time, our trainer called five freshers, including Manisha and me, out of the class room. Introducing us to a project lead who was working in mid-range technology, he told us, "I was asked to shortlist the names of the top five students of my class so that they may be accommodated in one of the best projects of mid-range technology. I gave your names. This gentleman will take you to the operations and development centre." We all went along with the project lead.

During the first day of my project, I was introduced to the whole team. I became part of a team that had fifteen offshore team members and three onsite team members. I met people of almost every age group. All of them were older than me. There were Tamilians, Malayalees, Bengalis and Punjabis in my team. I had never worked with such a cosmopolitan team before. I was a fresher, so it seemed a big challenge for me to adjust to people of different ages and backgrounds and work together as a team.

As the first week passed, I saw different aspects of professional life – a life I had hitherto not been exposed to. I noticed how people work, the technical terms they use in meetings and how sometimes, senior people shout at their juniors when they make mistakes. It was the learning phase of my career. And it was a coincidence that this was the beginning of my struggle in both my professional as well as my personal life.

Two weeks passed. One day when I was waiting for my office bus at the sector 22 market, I saw someone hiding behind a tree at the bus stop. I caught a glimpse of this person as he was peeping from behind the tree. I couldn't believe my eyes! It was Jaison! I smiled in excitement, "Jaison, is it really you?"

All in a gush Jaison said, "Chunnu, I can't even begin to tell you how I've spent my days without you. Of course, your parents declared our official break up. But don't you see we're still one and miss each other so badly. I haven't seen your face for so many days now. I was desperate and I knew I just had to see you. So I thought I would just look at you secretly. You would never even come to know about it. You'd told me earlier that you live in sector 22. I am in Palam Vihar which is pretty near your sector. Today I got up at seven thirty in the morning and came to see you. How are you, my love?"

I looked into his eyes, kissed him on his cheeks and said, "I miss you, sweetheart. I cannot live without you. Will you come to see me in the evening today? We'll meet here at the market."

Jaison said, "Yes, sweetheart."

My office bus arrived and I got into the bus. I waved to Jaison from the window and quickly blinked away my tears. We smiled at each other as the bus departed.

In the evening I waited for Jaison at the CCD coffee shop. He came in, a little late as usual. We found a small table in a corner and ordered coffee. We looked into each other's eyes. I could see so much of love in his eyes. We held hands.

I told Jaison, "It's impossible. I cannot break off this relationship." He said, "Same here." Together we said, "We will fight for us and get married because we can't live without each other." It was as if we had taken a sacred vow. It gave both of us courage.

After that, we continued to meet each other every evening at the sector 22 market and from there, we would visit The Pizza Corner in

Ansal Plaza at Palam Vihar. It was a small restaurant. Jaison was very fond of cheese, so he would order two pan pizzas and two cups of coffee. We would share our professional experiences and talk about ourselves. Then we would walk around the streets of Palam Vihar and look at the big houses in wonder.

One day we looked at a beautiful, red house and Jaison told me, "'One day we will live together is such a big house." I said, "I hope your dream comes true and that we can get married. I want a sweet little house. I'll decorate our house and cook for you. You'll simply love it." We hugged and looked at each other tenderly.

Weekends, we would visit malls and spend the whole day there. We would watch a movie, have lunch and dinner at the food court. But somewhere, all along, I was scared because of my brother. Fortunately, we never ran into him at the mall. I suppose it was because God was with us.

> As time passed, I started facing new professional challenges. I noticed how smart people were and played dirty politics to get promotions. There are two ways of climbing the career ladder. Either you perform well and get the promotion or you are smart and get close to your manager and get promoted. I, however, am a very straight forward person. I would rather say things directly than in a sugar coated manner.

My straight forward approach was disliked intensely by my seniors. Some of my batch mates, who had joined the team with me, built very good personal relationships with a few of our seniors. My project lead was more comfortable talking to boys so he always assigned me tasks that neither used my potential to the fullest nor gave me a chance to prove myself. One day, I couldn't take it any longer and asked him directly what the problem was. "Why aren't you assigning me tasks that can use my technical skills to the fullest? How will I grow in this project then? Also, if you just want to keep me for these low level tasks then I'd rather you did not include me in this project."

The project lead blamed me instead, "I notice you don't stay late at work and you also come very late to the office. You don't take any initiative from your side. Look at your colleagues, they stay late every day and do a lot of work. I replied, "Why should I stay late every day when I don't have work? I don't think it's necessary to pretend. Also, I think it spoils the work culture. Everyone should be efficient enough to finish their tasks from nine in the morning to six thirty in the evening. If people are not able to meet their deadlines within the estimated time, then that's a serious problem of productivity and planning. And one more thing, I never come late to the office. I come by the office bus so I always reach office on time. If you don't assign me any good work then how will you come to know about my technical skills?"

After that huge outburst, I felt very upset. I picked up my handbag and went back home. Those days, Jaison and I were not meeting every day because he had shift timings and had to spend a lot of time at the call centre. But on that day, I called him up to meet me in the evening as I was very upset with whatever had happened at office.

We met in a coffee shop at sector 22. I narrated the whole story to him. Jaison said, "It's your first job, so you don't know much about politics. I know all about it because I've been in so many organisations. But believe me, one day they'll recognise your talent and your merit and all their politics will fail. You don't worry about anything, just be yourself."

Between sips of piping hot coffee Jaison told me, "I am missing my mom very much so this weekend, I'll go to Chandigarh. I won't be able to meet you."

I said, "That's all right Jaison, but what will I do without you here?"

Jaison said, "Do one thing. Go meet your parents."

I stared at him and said, "You know I'm not talking to my family from the last few months. Whenever they call me, I shout at them because I feel so frustrated with them. I miss them but I can't go home because they will again start pressurising me to get married to someone else. They don't understand my feelings. They expect me to forget you and say 'yes' to whatever they want me to do. Not only that, they also want to see me happy. You tell me, how is it possible? I can't dream about going home."

Jaison said, "Tell me, how long can you live without them? I know you love your family very much. You should go and meet them. They are your parents, all said and done. They are also constrained by society like my mother. Maybe they will take a lot of time to understand your feelings for me and to understand how deep your love for me is. Anyway, think about it. It's getting late. You should leave now."

He dropped me at my PG and said goodbye.

I told Manisha that night that Jaison was going home the coming weekend. "He's asked me to visit my folks also."

Manisha said, "Come on, Naina, relax! Have some patience and stop worrying. Let's go to a mall and do some shopping."

I said, "Good idea! I've been to the mall several times with Jaison but I've never done any shopping with him. When we're together, we're more interested in only spending time with each other."

Manisha and I reached the Metropolitan Mall the following morning. I bought some formal clothes, a pair of shoes, a pair of jeans and two tops. I spent a lot of money. Girls always feel happy after spending a lot of money. My money is hard earned but I also felt happy after spending it so lavishly. Like most shoppers, both of us ate at the food court.

Jaison called me up at night, "Hey sweetheart, how are you? So, what's up?"

I said, "Today I did a lot of shopping. I'm happy."

"Okay, so what did you buy?"

"I bought a pair of trousers for seventeen hundred, jeans for a thousand, a pair of shoes cost me twelve hundred and two tops for about eleven hundred rupees," I rattled off happily.

Jaison said, "Wow! You've spent a lot of money! But I am happy for you because you sound happy. I know you've spent so much on your shopping for the first time in your life. Look at your progress, Chunnu! You're a small town girl who'd never bought a pair of shoes for more than a hundred bucks and a pair of jeans for no more than three fifty."

I smiled, "You're right, Jaison. Hey, you're sounding happy! It's because you're with your mother and sister. You've been staying away from home for the first time in your life.It 's obvious you miss your family badly."

Jaison said, "You're right, Chunnu. I miss them every day. For my love I left them all alone in Chandigarh. I am so selfish."

I said, "Don't blame yourself. Look at the positive side of this situation. You'll have so many new experiences while staying away from your family. You'll get to meet so many people and learn how to survive. This will only make you strong. Look at me, I'm doing the same thing, aren't I? Metropolitan cities have many more opportunities than our small cities and to grow in life, this is the only way. We aren't alone in doing this. There are millions of people who have similar stories. They have to leave their small towns and come to metro cities to make their lives."

We talked for an hour. After disconnecting the phone, I suddenly started missing my family very badly. I prayed to God, "Please solve all our problems. I have started this fight with my loved ones for my love. But I never wanted to fight with them. I trust you Lord, I am sure one day you will solve all my problems."

Manisha saw me crying and consoled me. She held my hand and said, "Don't cry Naina. You're a fighter and so bold. I know you'll be able to solve all your problems. Your parents will see the light one day. They'll support you. You'll get married to Jaison and have a great life together. If you miss your family, then go see them. I am going to Yamuna Nagar next week. Come with me. We'll leave on Saturday and come back on Sunday."

> Five months had passed since Jaison and I had been in Gurgaon. I started visiting Yamuna Nagar. But I wouldn't speak to anyone there. I would leave on Saturday and reach there in the afternoon. After that, I would sleep till the evening. Whenever my parents would try to talk to me about Jaison, I would go upstairs without answering them. The following day I would leave by a quarter to eleven. This way, I never gave my parents a chance to brainwash me even once. But it gave me a lot of satisfaction as I got the chance to see all of them once a month.

After a few more months in Gurgaon, one evening when Jaison and I were together, I found him looking frustrated. I asked him, "What's happened?"

Jaison said, 'I'm feeling frustrated with this stupid call centre job. I have no life, only sleepless nights and lonely days in a PG. I had a six month bond here. Now that I've completed my six months, I don't want to continue here anymore. I miss home very much. I left my mother and my sister all alone there for my selfish reasons. But I don't want to live here anymore. I've decided to resign and go back to Chandigarh."

I got irritated and shouted at him, "I'm not talking to my family because of our relationship. I wait for every weekend to spend some time with you. Now you are saying that you miss your family and you cannot survive any more in this call centre job. I know your job is not easy but you can't leave me all alone here just because you are frustrated. Tell me, can you resign without any other job in your hand? What will you do in Chandigarh? If you are planning to get married to me then you should not go back to Chandigarh. You should search for another job here. I want you to complete your MBA and settle down in your life. I know my parents are not happy with this inter-religious marriage but I don't want anyone to raise questions about your career. Why don't you think of it this way?"

Jaison was adamant, "See Naina, I can't stay here. I've decided to go back. I know I can also make my career in Chandigarh."

I said, "Jaison, you know you'll get better opportunities here in Gurgaon rather than in Chandigarh. Anyway, now it is none of my business. Do whatever you want to do. But I won't marry you until you get settled in life."

After this huge fight, I left for my PG.

At midnight Jaison called me up and said, "Chunnu, I know you're upset because I have decided to leave. I'm worried about my career, and that's why I want to go back for a better job. I'll come to see you once every month."

I said, "I'm sorry too. My love for you is intense. It blocks my mind and makes me say so many things. You're right. Life is getting tougher for me day by day. I am facing challenges both in my personal as well as my professional life. In Chandigarh we used to be together for the complete day. When we came to Gurgaon, we started meeting in the evenings and on weekends. Now you're going to Chandigarh and you'll come to see me once a month."

Jaison said, "We'll have to face this struggle. It will test our relationship. Very rarely do long distance relationships survive. If our love is true and strong, we will never get separated."

True to his word, Jaison resigned from the call centre and returned to Chandigarh. We called each other every day. After some days, he told me, "I'm getting frustrated. Fifteen days have already passed and till now, I haven't got any job offer. I've started preparing for the MBA exams to keep myself busy. I'm also completing my MBA assignment. I have to appear for my MBA exams after one week."

I reasoned with Jaison, "Don't feel frustrated. It was your decision to go back to Chandigarh. Don't worry. Everything happens for the good. You work hard this semester and pass your MBA exams. Remember at this point of time, the MBA is more important than getting a new job. Wish you all the best. I'll talk to you every day only for fifteen to twenty minutes so that you can concentrate on your studies."

After one week, Jaison appeared for his MBA exams. Once it got over, he prepared for the interview and got a job in an MNC in Chandigarh. He called me up to tell me the good news. I was happy for him but the package was not good enough. I asked him to keep trying, "One day you'll get your dream job with a good package."

> I was about to complete one year in Gurgaon and Jaison would visit me once every month. On Fridays he would travel through the night and reach Gurgaon on Saturday morning. In the morning, he would stay with his friend at his old PG, where he would pay for his one day stay. After resting for a while, he would spend the whole day with me in a shopping mall. In the evening, we would go to our favourite place - Pizza Corner - at Palam Vihar. The following morning Jaison would leave for Chandigarh.
>
> After one year, I was promoted from a software trainee to a software engineer. My pay package also increased. I had changed a lot within this one year. I had fallen in love, experienced progress and struggle in equal measure. I had moved from Yamuna Nagar to Chandigarh to Gurgaon. I wasn't a small town girl any more.
>
> Every month I spent between three thousand to five thousand rupees on my shopping. I became part of the big city crowd who wore branded clothes and spent a lot of their disposable income on their luxuries. I had no responsibility on my shoulders so I managed to save a bit and my bank balance looked healthy. I wanted to buy my own car because I did not want to travel in auto rickshaws and local buses any

more. I also wanted to prove to everyone in my family and to others that in spite of being a small town girl, I wasn't less than any man. I wanted to make my own place in society. I wanted to be independent and fulfil all my dreams. Jaison also supported me and gave me confidence that I would one day fulfil all my dreams.

One evening while I was talking to Jaison, my brother called up. My phone was engaged so my brother understood that I was probably talking to him. Priyanshu called up my parents and told them that I was still continuing to see Jaison. After sometime, my father called me up and asked me, "Naina, are you still in touch with Jaison?"

My silence spoke for me and my father understood everything. He said, "Why do you want to continue with that guy? Do you want to see us dead? It seems you have made up your mind to spoil our reputation by continuing an inter-religious affair. We want to talk to you. We're coming to meet you tomorrow. We will have to finish this matter."

I shouted back at them, "Don't come to meet me. I don't want to meet anyone. All of you stress me out and I don't want to go mad. I need peace in my life."

The following day I got a call from my father. He said, "Naina we've reached Gurgaon and we're staying at Priyanshu's place. We are coming to your PG in the next one hour and then we will talk to you."

I shouted at them, "What are you saying? I don't want to talk to you and don't come to my PG. Please don't create a scene here. I'm not going to leave Jaison. You can't force me to end this relationship. I am committed to him."

After two hours Priyanshu called me up and shouted at me, "You stupid girl! Mom has been hospitalized. Her stress level was so high that her blood pressure shot up. It's entirely your fault. If something happens to my mother then I will not leave that guy. I am telling you for the first and last time."

I started crying and praying for my mother. "God please save my mother. I can neither live without Jaison nor can I live without my mom. Please help me. I do not want to lose any one."

After sometime, I called up Priyanshu and asked, "How's mom?"

He was livid, "She's better now and I'm taking her to my place."

I was dying to see my mother. I could not stop myself from saying, "Priyanshu, please drop Mom and Dad to my place. I want them to stay at my place tonight. I don't want to see Mom in pain."

Priyanshu said, "I'll do that but you'll have to promise them that you'll break off your relationship with Jaison forever".

I had no choice but to disconnect the phone. After one more hour, my parents reached my place. My mother was looking very ill and lifeless. I could easily understand from her expression that she was really worried and sick. I took my parents to my room. My roommates were out for two days so there was enough space for three people. I locked my room from the inside. My parents hugged me and told me, "We are not your enemies. You have left your family just for one guy. Now you hardly come over and you don't even talk to us. We feel so bad for you. You have isolated yourself and you're struggling all by yourself. We want to be a part of your life but you have cut us out of your life. What's happened to you? Leave that guy."

I could not see them crying and promised them that I would leave Jaison. The following day my parents left for Yamuna Nagar.

Next day I called up Jaison and narrated the whole incident to him. He didn't know what to say. He simply asked me, "So are you leaving me again?"

I said, "I don't know Jaison but what I do know is that I love my family and you equally. I don't want to lose anyone. My mother was not well so I had to promise her that I would leave you."

> I had completed one and a half years in Gurgaon. I couldn't break up with Jaison and I continued to meet him. The unpleasantness between me and my parents continued. My mother's hypertension increased causing me a lot of anxiety. I kept praying to God for the wellbeing of my parents, Jaison and our relationship. I refused to take my brother's calls and he stopped calling me. Though I was in the same city, I never allowed my brother to visit me.
>
> One day, however, I came to know from my parents that Priyanshu had met with an accident while riding his motor bike. He was badly injured and had to be hospitalised. I wanted to cry when I heard this. I felt very sorry that I had not been able to help my brother. Though both of us were

> in the same city, I was not able to meet him even in his hour of need because of the differences that had cropped up between us.
>
> I was also exposed to a lot of politics in my professional life. A few of my batch mates, who had joined the project later, were given a chance to visit USA and work onsite. "And all because of internal politics," I realised. I confronted my manager and asked him outright why he didn't send me onsite.
>
> My manager replied, "We think you aren't skilled enough to go to onsite and handle the work there. We feel that your colleague is a better fit for this job than you are."
>
> I said, "If you think I'm not good enough even after one and half years, then why don't you leave me out of this project? Why do you still want to keep me on in this project?"
>
> He had no answer but finally he retorted, "You need to complete two years offshore and learn the support process to go to onsite."
>
> I had always learned to face challenges in life. I knew that the person who was being sent onsite was far less skilled than I was and did not know any support process. I promised myself, "One day, this manager will himself ask me to go to USA."
>
> Within two months I had learnt the support process so well that now every step was on my fingertips. I dispelled the manager's myth that I was less skilled than my colleague.

I realised that it was my bad luck that followed me everywhere and created obstacles - both in my personal as well as my professional life. But I never lost confidence in myself, belief in my capacity for hard work and faith in God.

After a few months, Jaison called me up one day and told me that he would be going to Chennai the following month, as he had been selected by an MNC located there.

I was shocked to hear that. "Why are you going so far away from me and your family? Recently you got another job in Chandigarh and now again you are switching? What's happened to you suddenly?"

Jaison said, “Chunnu, I want to increase my pay package and this company is giving me good money. I can earn more in this post by earning extra incentives. I am doing all this for our relationship. You know very well that I do not come from a rich background, so I will have to start building my bank balance for our future.”

I was heartbroken, “Oh dear God, why are you testing us so much? Now I don’t even know how frequently we will be able to meet.

Jaison said, “Yes, it will be difficult for both of us to accept this but we’ll have to live with it. I won’t be able to meet you every month now but I promise I’ll meet you once every three months. It takes three days by train to travel from Chennai to Delhi and I do not want to spend three days in the train so I have decided that I will travel by air to come to Gurgaon. That way I will save time and be able to spend the weekend with you. Air travel is expensive and it will erode our savings, so I’ve decided it has to be once in three months.”

After one month, Jaison came to meet me before going off to Chennai. We went to a mall and spent the whole day there, ate our lunch and dinner, watched a movie and discussed our future plans in the remaining time. When the day ended, we left the mall and reached our favourite place, Palam Vihar. We held hands and walked about, looking at the big houses there, as we had often done in the past. It was about nine o’clock when Jaison said, “Sweetheart, it’s getting late. You should go back to your PG now. I’ll leave for Chandigarh by the last bus tonight and tomorrow, I’ll leave for Chennai.”

It was dark and we stood on the roadside under the trees. I clung to him – it was as if I was frightened to let him go. I froze in his arms and it seemed I would fall down unconscious. Jaison held me close. He felt so worried, he didn’t know what to do. He patted me on my cheeks gently, until I came back to my senses. He asked me tenderly, “What’s happened to you Chunnu? I’m not going forever. I’ll come to meet you. Chennai is not all that far from here. Please don’t be like this. It hurts me.”

He hugged me tightly and kissed me on my forehead. Then he dropped me back to my PG and left for Chandigarh.

Jaison reached Chennai in the next four days. I couldn’t talk to him much in those four days because of roaming and network issues on his cell phone.

After some days he called me up, "Chunnu, how are you? I'm missing you a lot."

I loved hearing his voice again. "Hi, Jaison, how are you? Have you settled down?"

"Yes, you know, Chennai is a totally different place. I don't know Tamil so I'm finding it very difficult to communicate with people over here. I've got a one bedroom flat and I'll be sharing this accommodation with a North Indian fellow."

I was relieved. "Do you like your new office?"

"Yes, I've joined the new office and so far, so good. I find the work more challenging here. My office is in Guindy. But the food….." his voice trailed off.

"Why what's wrong with the food?"

"I'm getting tired of the food! Every day I have to eat dosas and idlis. I know, I know, my parents are from South India, but Chunnu, I've been born and brought up in Punjab. I prefer Punjabi food. By the way Chunnu, I've got a new phone connection. You can call me on my new number."

> As time passed, the phone calls became infrequent as Jaison became busy with his work. Now he could not give me that much time. I continued to struggle in my career in office and for the sake of my love and my family. I had now completed two years in Gurgaon. I had started feeling lonely without Jaison. Everything had seemed rosy for two years. Now the fights started between us.

One day, when he called me up, I started shouting at him, "Thank God you've got the time to call me. You hardly talk to me for fifteen to twenty minutes a day and then you feel sleepy because your new job is so demanding. Now tell me what I should do. You can't meet me every day or even once a month. I have to wait for three months to see you. Above all this, I can't even go home every weekend because my parents pressurise me to get married to the boy of their choice. Even though I am in the same city, I don't meet my brother because he hates our relationship. Now tell me, why am I living this life? Every day has become a challenge for me. For me, weekends are black days. Tell me, what should I do? Why did you go to Chennai? You could have found a job here also."

He listened to my outburst patiently but couldn't control himself at the end, "Stop this. You know, I can't help it. You'll have to survive like this only. I haven't asked you to stop talking to and meeting your family. I'm also not enjoying here all by myself. My destiny has brought me here. I also miss my family. But I don't cry like you."

I banged the phone down in anger. Then I waited for one hour. I thought he would call me back. But he didn't. I had to call him back. No one picked up the phone. After almost ten missed calls, he said in sleepy voice, "Hello……"

I was perplexed by his behaviour. "Jaison, you were actually asleep! How can you sleep so blissfully after a fight? It means you just don't care about me. Here I couldn't sleep because I was feeling bad after our fight."

Jaison replied calmly, "I was tired, so I slept. You need to be a little mature. We cannot fight over small things. You'll have to accept the fact that we cannot talk so much every day because there is a lot of work pressure. See I'm sorry, Chunnu. I love you. Please don't feel bad about anything. Pray to God that one day we get married and live together forever. Then we won't have to cry to spend a few minutes with each other."

His words soothed me. I said, "I love you too. Good night."

I wanted to enjoy my life in Gurgaon in spite of these difficult phases in my life. I got a nice group of friends both in my PG and as well as in my office. In my paying guest accommodation, there was one girl named Heena who was employed in a BPO. She had a boyfriend who was from Maharashtra whereas, she was from North India. Like me, she was also facing difficulties in her family. They did not approve of this alliance.

I realise now that many girls who leave their home towns and stay away from their families have stories that are more or less similar. But unlike me, Heena was enjoying her life to the fullest because her boyfriend was in the same city. Manisha and I were also acquainted with Heena and her boyfriend. We became good friends. One weekend, all the girls made a plan to go to a discotheque. Manisha, Heena and I had never been to a discotheque before. Heena told me that only couples could visit 'discs' but she also added, "I know there's a disc in Sahara Mall where we can go in a group."

I said, "The disc will open late at night. We are all girls, then how will we go there without a male escort?"

Heena assured us, 'Don't worry, I've already spoken to my boyfriend. He'll come with us. He has also arranged a çar for us. So there'll be no problem in commuting."

Manisha and I were excited, "Ok then, we are all set to go!"

All of us dressed in black outfits and wore a lot of makeup.

Heena said, "Girls, he'll come to pick us at ten thirty. So come, let's get ready to rock!"

We had our dinner and got ready. Heena's boyfriend came to pick us from our PG. He looked at us and said, 'Wow girls, you're all looking stunning today."

We reached Sahara Mall and took a lift to the top floor. Two bouncers were standing outside the discotheque. They asked how many of us wanted to go in. One of the men put a stamp on the back of our hands and took the entry fee from each one of us. Only then did he allow us to enter the night club. It was dark inside and there was a bar and a snacks counter in one corner. The discotheque was divided into two parts. One part had a dance floor while the other part had a small restaurant where people were enjoying drinks and food. The music playing there was very loud, in fact it was deafening. Heena ordered non-alcoholic drinks for all of us. While we were enjoying our soft drinks, Heena's boyfriend pulled her to the dance floor and started dancing to Shakira's latest numbers.

There at the nightclub, I missed Jaison a lot. I told Manisha, "When I was in Chandigarh I had asked Jaison many times to take me to a night club. But he would always refuse. According to him, it wasn't a suitable place for girls.

Manisha laughed, "Does he know that it's past midnight and his girl is sitting in a night club?"

I replied confidently, "Don't worry. I'll tell him and I'm sure he won't say anything to me."

Suddenly Heena pulled me and Manisha to the dance floor. I started dancing to the songs of Dil Chahta Hai and other Punjabi numbers. Everyone seemed to be in high spirits. As the night progressed, many more couples came to the night club. Each girl was dressed differently.

Even the newly married girls wore short skirts, tube tops and red chooras (red bangles worn by Punjabi girls after marriage). Some of the perfumes the girls and boys had used were very heady and the smell mixed with the stale odour of cigarettes gave me a headache. Colourful laser and strobe lights flashed on the people on the dance floor. Smoke billowed out from the corners as if in sync with the drum beats. At around two thirty, we decided to go back to our PG accommodation. We enjoyed a lot that night but I never disclosed to my family that I had gone to a discotheque.

After a few more months, one day at the team meeting in office, my project lead announced that I would be the next one to be sent onsite. And that I should be ready with my passport and visa in the next two months. This certainly was news for me! This was the only thing that filled me with happiness. Otherwise, the last two years had been so difficult. Everyone in the team congratulated me. It was like a dream come true for me and I was on cloud nine. I could not believe that I had done it. At least my hard work had paid off. My struggle seemed worth it.

I wanted to share this piece of news with my family and Jaison. I forgot all my fights and called my parents excitedly. My mother picked up the phone.

"Hello Ma, how are you?"

I heard my mother's voice after a long time. She sounded anxious, "I'm fine. Is everything alright with you there?"

I replied, "Yes Ma, everything's good. I want to tell you something."

I could feel the tension mounting in her voice, "What's happened?"

I replied, "Mom, I'm going to USA in the next two months."

My mother was overjoyed, she said, "God bless you my child. Today you have done something that no one else has done in your family. You have made a lot of progress in life. You have achieved so much in your life even though you have faced difficulties because you're a girl. We worked hard for you kids and today our kids have made us proud. I'm so proud of you. I'm sure that in life you'll be very successful. Your father will be very happy when I tell him. My child, you've never taken a flight. How will you manage to travel overseas all alone? Where will you live and what will you eat there?"

I was overwhelmed, "Thanks Mom. What you've just told me means a lot to me. And don't you worry about me. I'll manage everything. My friends, who are already living in USA, will arrange accommodation for me and there are so many Indian stores there, I'll also get good Indian food. Don't worry about me."

I called up Jaison after I had spoken to my mother, "Hi Jaison, what were you doing?"

"Nothing really. Just came back from office. I was going to a restaurant nearby to eat my dinner."

"Guess what?"

Of course Jaison couldn't have imagined what I was going to tell him next. He asked, "What?"

I paused and then told him excitedly, "I'm going to USA."

Jaison said, "Wow! That's great! I'm so proud of you. I knew that one day your hard work will bring good news for you and see it's already happening. You're such a determined girl. Once you make up your mind to get something, you really work hard to get it. Do you realise how happy your parents will be?"

I said, "Yes, I called up my mother today and told her. She was very happy."

Jaison asked, "So Naina, how are you feeling at this moment?"

I said, "I've no words to describe my feelings. Till now I've only visited a few places. This will be the longest journey of my life and that too on board a flight."

Jaison comforted me, "Don't worry about your journey and your stay there. Both will be good. This will be the best time of your life. I wish you all the best."

After a few days, I applied for a visa through my company and was called by the US embassy for the interview. My senior colleagues gave me many instructions and tips about attending the interview. A few days later, I received my passport with the US visa stamped in it. My company booked my flight tickets.

I called up my parents to tell them that I had got my tickets. My father spoke to me tenderly, "My dear little daughter, I'm so happy for you. I've told everyone in office that my daughter is going to USA. My colleagues' children haven't made their parents so proud. I have also told my brothers and sisters about your trip. Everyone is so happy for you. They couldn't believe that a girl from our family would be able to go to USA. I have even shared this news with our friends and neighbours."

I said, "Thanks Dad! I can understand your happiness."

My father said, "Send me an email with your flight details. Your mom, your brother and I will come to drop you to the airport. Bye and may God bless you."

I started making preparations for my journey. I spent so much to buy clothes, shoes and bags for myself.

Two months passed and my date of travel drew near. Jaison planned to meet me before that. One week before my travel date, he flew down to Delhi to see me.

He reached sector 22, Gurgaon at five in the morning and called me up. I picked up the phone and my voice thick with sleep said, "Hello."

Jaison said, "Good morning Chunnu. You're still sleeping and here I'm dying to see you. Get up and come down, I'm waiting for you at the main gate. Come quickly, I've got something for you."

I went downstairs but the main gate was locked. Jaison was standing outside. We looked at each other and smiled. He said, "This is for you, Chunnu." He had a small gift in his hands. He handed it to me through the iron bars of the door. I took it, opened the packet and there was a little golden Ganesha inside. I gave him a flying kiss and said, "Thanks dear. It's so beautiful. I'll keep it with me till the end of my days."

Jaison said, "Take it with you when you go to the US. God will always help you in difficulties. This is my blessing for you. Now go back to sleep. I am going to Palam Vihar and will stay at my old PG. We'll meet around ten thirty and then we'll go to the mall and spend a nice day together."

I went back to sleep and then at nine thirty, got up, took a bath, had my breakfast and got ready to meet Jaison. He met me at the sector 22 market. From there we went to the shopping mall.

I said, "Jaison, I'm glad you've hired an auto rickshaw to go to the mall. I know it's expensive but it's much better than going in a crowded bus. I hate to travel in a local bus and sit with people who don't have the decency to sit next to a girl."

"I care for you," Jaison said tenderly, "and that's why I didn't want to take you in that bus."

I said, "I know. But you know what, that's not the only problem. On rainy days I hate to cross flooded roads to catch my office bus. I've decided that after I come back from the US, I'll buy a car and not take a single paisa from my parents."

Jaison said, "Wow! Now that would really be great. I'm sure you'll be able to do this."

We went to the mall and spent the whole day there.

At night Jaison and I hired an auto rickshaw to come back to sector 22. In the rickshaw Jaison said, "Naina, now I realise how bad you must've felt when I left for Chennai. After a few days, you'll go out of the country and then it'll be impossible for me to meet you. I'm feeling very depressed at this moment."

I snuggled close to him. "Don't get upset. I'll be back soon. Think about our families," I said, trying to lighten his mood, "they must be quite relieved to know we won't be able to meet for some time." Jaison smiled.

"I'll enjoy my stay there," I continued, "you know, after one and half months, Manisha will join me there and we'll be living together".

Jaison looked relieved, "That's great. Manisha is your roommate here and you are comfortable with her. When she joins you there your life will become easier. Then you won't need to live with someone you're not familiar with."

We reached sector 22. Jaison hugged me tightly and kissed me. He wished me all the best for my journey and left for Chennai. I reached my PG.

Now only one day was left for my trip. My roommates helped me to pack my bags. I wrapped all the gifts given by Jaison, a small statue of Goddess Durga, some holy books and the golden Ganesha and kept them in my cabin bag. The following day my parents and Priyanshu arrived at my PG to drop me to the Indira Gandhi International airport at New Delhi. My brother was glad to see me going. He hugged me. My parents were happy but they started crying as for the first time in their life I was going so far from them. They blessed me and wished me all the best.

> I was going to travel by air for the first time and that too by British Airlines, which I believe is among the world's best airlines. I was excited but also nervous. When I saw the airport for the first time, my heart started beating fast. I will never forget that experience - it was a surreal moment for me. My nervousness peaked as I entered the air-conditioned airport. In a flash my mind raced back to those days when we used to travel in the inexpensive general compartment of the Indian railways where every person jostled with his fellow passenger for a bit of space. I have never forgotten the blistering hot air stinging my soft cheeks when I looked out of the train window during our journeys to my maternal grandmother's house in the hot sunny days of June.

The security personnel at the main gate checked my passport before allowing me to enter the airport. I saw people moving around but I didn't know what to do next. I saw beautiful girls dressed in short, tight shirts. They were talking sweetly to people and offering them help.

One of them came to me and asked, "Which airlines are you flying Ma'am and where are you going?" For two seconds I just looked at her lips, she was wearing a bold red shade of lipstick. Red is one of my favourite colours.

I concealed my nervousness and tried to sound casual, "I'm going to New York by British Airways."

She said, "Ma'am, please proceed to counter number I9 to check in your baggage and for your security check."

I moved to counter 19. The beautiful and well turned out woman at the counter asked me to keep my baggage on the weighing machine.

After checking in my luggage, I took my cabin bag and handbag and moved for the security check. This was my very first experience of international travel and my nervousness was evident. My hands shook so much that I dropped my passport twice. The person sitting at the immigration counter noticed my discomfiture and said, "Kya ho gaya madamji? passport kyon gira rahe ho? Jo kho gaya to dikkat ho javegi. (What's happened madam? Why you are dropping your passport? Be careful, should you lose it you'll face a lot of trouble)." I took a deep breath and tried to calm myself. After the immigration check, I heard the announcement, “Passengers travelling to New York via London are requested to complete their security check and proceed towards the aircraft through gate number 7.” I kept my boarding pass in my pocket and ran towards gate number 7 as I didn’t want to miss the flight.

I followed the signs and reached gate number 7. While I was walking, my cell phone rang. I picked it up without looking at the number on the screen.

It was Priyanshu, “Hi Naina, Dad wants to talk to you.”

Dad took the phone and started talking, “Naina, we’re standing outside the airport and waiting for your flight to take off. We’ll see your plane take off and then leave.” My loving parents didn’t want to miss a single moment of my happiness.

I told him sweetly, “Dad, are you crazy? Several flights take off at any one moment. How will you recognise my airplane in the sky? You should leave for home. Don’t worry about me, please. I’ll be just fine.”

I walked out of the gate and approached the aircraft through a jet bridge. As I stepped inside, a British air hostess greeted me “Welcome ma’am. Please show me your boarding pass.” I was pleasantly surprised to hear someone twice my age call me ‘Ma’am’.

She took my boarding pass, glanced at it and said, “23A Ma’am…on your right.” I was entering an aeroplane for the first time in my life and for the first time ever, I was looking at the inside of a plane. It was clean with blue interiors and smelt fresh and oh-so-different from the local buses, auto rickshaws and trains that I was used to travelling in till now. All the people seemed so sophisticated.

There were two rows of seats with an aisle in between. I looked at the seats. They were plush and huge, almost as big as sofas. I quickly jumped into one though I was doubtful whether it was my seat. It looked like a business class seat while on my boarding pass, economy class was mentioned. An air hostess approached me and asked, “Do you need anything Ma’am?”

I gave her a blank look and told her, “I’m looking for 23A.”

She replied, “Ma’am, 23A is economy class and a little ahead.”

Embarrassed, I quickly said, “Oh! I’m sorry.” I left that comfortable seat and got up to search for 23A. Economy class is not comfortable for a journey of fourteen hours because one can only sit in one position and it becomes very cramped. I took my seat next to the window. When all the passengers had taken their seats, two air hostesses sprayed something from aerosol cans inside the aircraft. The thought struck me that we don't care for anyone's health when we travel in heavily crowded buses and trains. I wondered if this was one of the reasons why a flight is always more expensive than any other mode of transport. After a few minutes, another air hostess came and she gave us wet, disposable towels to wipe our hands with.

I watched all the demonstrations given by the airhostess very carefully. The seat belt sign had been switched on so I put on the seat belt. For me everything was new, so much so, that when I tried to use the touch screen to switch on the tiny television set in front of me, the passenger next to me had to inform me that it would start only after the plane had taken off.

A few minutes later, the plane took off. I clutched my stomach tightly expecting to feel queasy. My mother had warned me that people feel pain and discomfort in their stomachs and their ears get blocked when the plane takes off. I was almost deaf when the plane started gaining height. I looked out of the window and to my amazement, everything on earth had turned into tiny dots. Within moments of that, even the dots had faded and there were only clouds all around the plane. I was wonderstruck at that sight and at the thought of being so many thousands of feet above the ground.

Television screens came alive. Information regarding altitude, distance and the temperature outside was displayed on the screen. I started changing channels and stopped when I found a Hindi movie. After a few hours, I felt tired and wanted to recline my seat but I didn't know how to do it. I was a little hesitant to ask my co-passenger but I asked him anyway, as I didn't have any other choice. He showed me a button on the inner side of my chair and I was able to adjust my backrest. I thanked him a little shyly, embarrassed because I didn't know how to do it.

After several hours, my flight landed at the London airport. I looked out of the window and the view outside was absolutely amazing. I cannot express the feelings that were rushing through my mind at that moment. It was as if scenes from my childhood had started playing in reverse on the screen of my mind. I remembered my father's struggles. In my childhood, who could have imagined that one day I would travel overseas and that my family would feel so proud of me? Humbly, I thanked God for making it possible.

When I stepped down at London Heathrow airport, I felt all alone in a strange land where everything was new for me. I took a deep breath and stretched my arms towards the sky and embraced my new found independence. I felt happy.

I got into a bus to reach another terminal to catch the connecting flight to New York. I followed the sign boards at the airport and after the security check, started walking towards the gate from where my flight was to take off. I could not believe that I was walking in one of the biggest international airports of the world. I could smell the foreign perfumes and cosmetics in the duty free shops selling liquor, cosmetics, chocolates, clothes, souvenirs and many more things. I was wide eyed at this whole new experience and Yamuna Nagar seemed far away. I couldn't help but admire the beauty of the English girls who I thought looked like angels. No wonder our Indian boys run after these beauties. I saw couples holding hands and kissing each other passionately without being conscious of the people nearby. Well, I guess this happens in India too but not so openly.

I went into a cosmetic store. It was very big and had glossy lip shades in many colours on display. 'Try me' was written on some of the lipsticks. My lips were a little dry, so I tried a lipstick, sprayed some perfume on my clothes and headed towards my flight.

While waiting for my next flight, I realised that there was not a single Indian who was going from London to New York. For a minute I felt lonely and missed my country and its people. It's true, many times we criticise our country but we miss it and its people all the same, especially when we are strangers in a foreign land. After an hour, I caught the flight to New York. I was very tired and wanted to stretch my legs but that wasn't possible in economy class.

After a few hours, my flight landed at JFK airport in New York. I cleared all the immigration formalities, collected my baggage and reached the exit of the terminal. There, as instructed by my colleagues, I booked a share taxi to Stamford city. An American lady sitting across the ground transportation counter booked a shuttle taxi for me and asked me to wait for twenty minutes. I took a seat and looked outside the glass doors. The roads of New York were broad and clean. There were many taxis outside and the people waiting there were so very patient and well behaved. I was already missing the pushing and the shoving and the noisy environment of India. From our childhood we are used to crowds, chaos and noise. After a few minutes, the shuttle taxi arrived and the American lady called me. I got into the taxi and was surprised when the friendly taxi driver greeted me pleasantly. He seemed to be quite a knowledgeable person and all through the ride kept talking to me about cricket, my studies, my job and many other subjects.

Finally, I reached my destination and my long awaited dream came true. I was struck by the beauty of USA. Stamford seemed out of some fairy tale. I reached my friends' apartment on Strawberry Hill Avenue. My friends had cooked rajma and rice for me which I ate heartily not having had familiar food since I left India. I used their phone to call up Jaison and my parents. I told them that USA was beautiful - the roads were broad, the country was so clean, the people were helpful, there was no noise, no dust, no pollution.

I lived in USA for three months. During my visit, I went to see New York with my friends. This was the most exciting trip of my life. I caught a train from Stamford. Within forty five minutes, we reached the Grand Central Station. It is huge and the architecture is very imposing. Walking through the Grand Central is like walking through a museum housing works of art. There was a big enquiry booth and a ticket counter in the centre of the concourse. There were many exits in the station which led to the subways. People from all over the world could be seen at this one place. During peak hours, this becomes the most hectic place. I saw many tourists busy taking photographs of the station. I took a few photos of the beautiful art work myself. We bought some 'Dunkin Donuts' and coffee from Grand Central. I told my friends excitedly, "Hey, some Hindi movies have been shot at this station. Remember, how Shah Rukh Khan and Rani Mukherjee used to meet here at the Grand Central in Kabhi Alvida Na Kehna? I can almost imagine him singing here!"

We came out of the station and started walking. New York is so well organised. It has streets that are sequentially numbered – 41st Street, 42nd Street and so on. I thought it was one of the best places in the world. People could be seen roaming aimlessly on the roads – it seemed they had come just to enjoy their days and nights in New York. We reached Times Square which was surrounded by high rise buildings. I saw huge billboards with digital screens advertising well known products. Times Square was brightly illuminated, glamorous, an incredible sight which I could only see, feel and experience but not adequately convey to anyone back home.

There were many vendors selling ladies bags, gloves and woollens for just ten dollars. It reminded me of the Sunday market near my aunt's house in R.K. Puram, Delhi. These street vendors were mostly Indians, Pakistanis, Japanese or Africans. One African vendor tried to sell me a ladies bag for twenty five dollars.

I said, "Hey, everyone's selling it for ten dollars, why are you charging me twenty five?"

He tried his sales pitch on me, "It's very good quality. I'll give you a discount of five dollars and you can take it for twenty.

I haggled with him, "No it's too much."

Not one to give up, he asked, "Ok, then tell me how much do you want to pay?"

I said, "I'll pay only ten dollars."

The vendor asked me, "Where are you from?"

I replied, "I'm from India."

The vendor told me rudely, "Ok, then go back to India and buy it from there."

I was shocked to hear his words. It reminded me of the local market of Yamuna Nagar where shopkeepers speak in the same tone. I laughed and told the vendor, "Ok, no problem. I'll buy it from India."

I went to see Brooklyn Bridge, Central Park, Lexington Avenue, Empire State Building, the Statue of Liberty and many other places. It was like a dream come true for me. I could never have imagined that I would ever visit one of the most famous places in the world. At night I stood in the middle of Times Square and looked around. There were bright lights, big showrooms, music and a lively crowd all around me. Some people were dancing on the road, some people were painting with spray paint cans creating fascinating street art unique to New York, while others were selling hot dogs and burgers. Yellow taxi cabs were cruising along picking up passengers. Some people were taking photographs. To my surprise, one girl was even selling kisses and hugs for just a few dollars. "Wow, everything's for sale," I thought, "you can do whatever you like! It's the best place to relax. Just sit on the road side with a hot coffee, a blueberry muffin in your hand and enjoy life."

I turned my eyes and stretched my arms to the sky and said humbly, "Thank you God, for giving me a chance so that I could actually see this beautiful place. I feel I'm very, very lucky indeed. There are many people in this world who are not fortunate enough to spend such a lovely evening at such a beautiful place. But you gave me this opportunity. I'm really thankful to you and my parents who gave me these lovely moments in my life." I closed my eyes and said, "I'll always treasure these beautiful moments."

Within three months, I visited many places with my friends. I enjoyed my stay to the fullest and even did a lot of shopping.

Finally it was time to return to India. I called up Jaison and he said, "I am so happy Chunnu, as now I'll meet you after a long time. I'll come to see you when you are back. I love you a lot. Bon voyage and have a safe flight."

I returned to India. My family came to receive me at the airport. My parents and brother hugged me tight and there were tears in their eyes.

They took me to Yamuna Nagar for one week. I had already applied for leave from USA itself. I had come back after a long stay away from home. The following day, I received calls from all our relatives and our neighbours. In a typical fashion they told me, "So foreign returned Madam, now you won't like Yamuna Nagar as you've seen USA. Yamuna Nagar is much too small as compared to USA, isn't it?"

"Did they really seek confirmation from me?" I wondered. Aloud I replied, "I love Yamuna Nagar. I was born and brought up here. Wherever I may go in life, my heart and happiness will be in this small town for all times. It's true that I want to see life beyond Yamuna Nagar but it is this town which has made my life, so in my eyes, Yamuna Nagar is the best."

The first day passed with a lot of happiness and contentment all around. The following day I felt that my life was back on the same track because my parents started asking about Jaison and me once again. But this time, it seemed that their mindset had changed. They asked me, "Do you really want to marry Jaison? This marriage will not be that simple. You will have to sacrifice your religion, your culture and everything else that is familiar. Your life will become very difficult. You should think about it."

I said, "Please don't start all over again. I don't want to talk about this topic."

My father said, "How long will you continue this way? You're twenty five now and it's high time that you got married. Girls of your age are getting married. Everyone says that girls should get married at the right age otherwise they end up getting men who are divorcees or men who are twice their age. We want to end this matter now. Do you still want to get married to Jaison? I suggest that you don't go ahead because he isn't a suitable match for you."

I burst into tears and replied, "Dad, you won't understand our relationship. There is a bond between us. Tell me something, suppose I ask you to leave mother will you do so?"

My father had no answer. He struck his hand on his forehead and said, "We are your parents Naina and we'll always think for your good. But we cannot see you in pain any more. The final decision will be yours and you'll have to take full responsibility."

I could not believe my ears! My family had finally agreed to our relationship after three years. It seemed too good to be true. But then I realised that this agreement was only one sided. Jaison had not disclosed this matter to any of his relatives and their consent was more important than that of his mother's.

I told my parents that my decision was final. I would marry only Jaison. I asked them to meet him once.

One week later, I joined office back and I also changed my PG accommodation as I had to leave my old PG before going to USA.

Everyone in my team was happy to see me back. I had brought some chocolates from USA and distributed them among the team members. It seemed to me that after the trip I had become a bit of a hero in everyone's eyes and enhanced my position in office among my colleagues.

A few days later, I started my research on the internet about which car I should buy. While I was at home, I had learnt driving from a driving school. When I told my parents that I wanted to buy a brand new car for myself, they were very happy. My father suggested that I should buy a second hand car for myself because that would cost less. "That's so typical of him", I thought to myself, "Dad has always bought second hand things because he has never been in a comfortable financial situation."

I said to my father, "Second hand things always cost less at the outset when you buy them but their maintenance cost is very high. Things have changed Dad. Change your mindset and think big now."

After a few days, I finally booked a small car. It was Christmas so I got a good discount. When I was going to buy the car, I called up Priyanshu and he came to help me. We reached a car agency in Gurgaon and the car dealer enthusiastically showed us different models. Priyanshu and I looked at each other and smiled. We touched the shiny new cars lovingly and felt that we were indeed the happiest persons in the world. We remembered the day when we had attended a birthday party hosted by a rich man for his son's birthday. The son was my father's student. We had gone on my father's scooty while the other invitees had come in their big shiny cars.

Priyanshu told me, "For us, times have changed, sister. Now things are not the same. We are not rich but we are at such a position in our lives that we can buy any luxury for ourselves, do whatever we want, eat wherever we want, buy stylish clothes or even go wherever we want. Yet, how can we ever forget the days when our parents were struggling to buy us even small things for our happiness? Life sure is a roller coaster ride. It's so very unpredictable, bringing you both joy and grief. I'm so proud of you, Sis. You're the only one in our family who's covered such a long distance in such a short span of time."

After completing all the formalities, the dealer handed the car keys to me. I took it and my eyes filled with tears of joy. I told Priyanshu, "You're a better driver than I am. I want you to drive our new car to my PG."

Priyanshu replied, "Sure, but you should try your hands on the new car first. I'll drive after you."

I grasped the steering wheel in my hands and turned on the ignition key. I was a little nervous and found it difficult to control the car. My brother laughed and said, "I'm scared what you'll do on the roads. You need a lot of practice and I'll help you. He took the keys from me and drove the car to a 'Shani' temple in sector-14. There a swami ji did the puja, after which Priyanshu drove us to my PG.

For the next two days, I practised driving my new car. My brother also came to help me.

One day, while driving to office, I reached Kapashera border which was possibly one of the worst stretches in Gurgaon. It seemed that all the pedestrians walked on the street while vehicles moved on the footpath. Everyone was always in a hurry to reach their destination. Pedestrians walked in front of vehicles. Even if someone drove in first gear, he would probably hit someone and cause an accident. Being a beginner, I found it very difficult to drive at such a place. I tried to cross the border in first gear. But I did not know how to press the clutch and the accelerator in synchronization and my car kept stopping in the middle of the road. I started it again and tried to move forward. Many people were walking in front of my car. Suddenly, the front tyre of my car went over a person's foot. He cried out in pain and his ankle started bleeding. I panicked when I saw, what seemed to me, hundreds of people gathered around my car. People started banging on my car. Suddenly a policeman came and started beating the people who had gathered there. He then knocked on the car window. I rolled the window down. The policeman, who seemed to be from Haryana, told me, "Madam, car side me lagao. Apna licence dikhao. Madam ji aap chinta mat karo. Hum settlement kar lenge. Konsi company mein kaam karte ho aap? Shaadi ho gayi hai apki ya phir Gurgaon mein akele rehte ho?" (Madam, please park your car to one side and show me your driving licence. Don't worry, we'll settle this matter. Which company do you work in? Are you married or do you live in Gurgaon all by yourself?)

I replied, "I'm single and I work in an IT company nearby. I handed over my licence to the policeman and gave him my office address. I felt frightened and unnerved by the whole incident and my hands shook while I drove back to office.

I recounted the incident to a colleague in the 'admin' department of my company. He could see that I was in a bad shape and asked me to calm down reassuring me all the while that he would solve the matter.

After some time, two policemen came to the office and demanded some payment from me to settle the matter. When I gave them the money, one of the policemen started laughing, "Arrey madam ki halat to patli ho gayi thi. Madam ki height chhoti ho gayi thi dar ke marey. Wahan to hum time pe aa liye aur case ka rafa dafa kar diya, nahi to wo sarey to gaddi ki aisi taisi kar dete (Madam was so scared. It seemed as if she had shrunk out of panic. We reached there on time and saved her, otherwise those people would have broken the car)." I narrated this incident to a colleague in office and he started laughing at me. He told everyone that I had killed one person at the border and the police was searching for me. This became a joke for everyone in the office. Even my onsite team members called me up to make fun of me.

Within a few days, I started driving the car properly. I faced difficulty in reversing and parking but after a few trials I was able to do it. Everyone in the office congratulated me for my new car and asked for a party. I gave them a nice party in a restaurant in Metropolitan Mall.

When I called up Jaison and shared my happiness with him, he congratulated me. I asked him to learn driving. He was skeptical, "But why should I learn driving?"

I replied, "Because after marriage we both will have to drive this car." He asked incredulously, "What are you saying?"

I replied, "Yes Mr. Jaison, my parents have finally agreed to meet you."

Jaison said, "Wow, now that's something! Sure, I'll meet them. Let's meet next week. I will fly down to Delhi and together, we'll go to Yamuna Nagar."

I was only too happy to hear this. I discussed it with Priyanshu and he agreed to come along.

That weekend, Priyanshu came to my PG and drove the car to the airport to pick up Jaison. Priyanshu was going to meet Jaison for the first time in his life and even though Jaison had come to meet me in Gurgaon many times, Priyanshu had never managed to catch him.

Priyanshu hugged Jaison and was respectful towards him. On our way from Delhi to Yamuna Nagar, Priyanshu started questioning Jaison about his job, his family and lifestyle. I understood that Priyanshu was trying to gauge his temperament and analyse his personality traits. They were sitting in front while I sat on the back seat. I knew what Priyanshu was up to and I was a little scared as one wrong answer could change Priyanshu's mind forever. On the way we stopped at Nilkantha dabha where we had big glasses of tea with tandoori aloo paratha with lots of white butter. After the meal when Priyanshu went to wash up, I got a chance to talk to Jaison.

I said, "Be careful with your answers as Priyanshu is trying to analyse you." Jaison grinned, "I'm a salesman and I know what he is trying to do. So don't worry about anything. I know what I have to say."

Priyanshu came back after five minutes and we reached Yamuna Nagar in the next two and a half hours.

I rang the doorbell and was surprised to see all my uncles and aunts at home as during my school days everyone had started living separately and they would visit Yamuna Nagar only during the summer vacations. Everyone welcomed Jaison and took him to the living room.

I felt angry with my parents. I took my mother to a corner and asked her, "Why have you called everyone? This is the matter of my marriage and why do you need everyone's approval before you say 'yes' to the boy."

My mother replied, "You cannot forget that once upon a time, we all lived together as a joint family, so whoever gets married requires an approval from every family member. We had already informed everyone and all of them have agreed to it. This way, at least no one will be an obstacle in your marriage. They are all ok with it. They say as Naina is standing on her own feet, she knows very well what is good or bad for her. So they have nothing to say."

My elder uncle asked Jaison, "So do you belong to Kerala or to Chandigarh?"

Jaison replied, "I was born and brought up in Chandigarh but my parents belong to Kerala. Many years ago my Dad came to Chandigarh from Kerala and he got a government job here. Then he met my mother who is also from Kerala. They got married and a few years later they constructed their own house in Chandigarh. They've been in Chandigarh for the last thirty years now."

My second uncle asked, "So where are your relatives and what do they do?"

Jaison replied, "A few of my uncles are in Chandigarh and the other relatives are in Kerala. They live a very simple life there. They have their own property there."

Then my youngest uncle asked, 'What did you like about Naina and why do you want to marry her?"

Jaison replied, "She's very simple at heart and a very bright girl. She is also very ambitious and above all this, she loves her family very much. When she told me about her parents' struggle then I realised that her life is similar to mine and so we'll understand each other throughout our lives. That's why I decided to marry her."

After all these questions and answers, my father said, "I want to finish off this matter soon because Naina is already 25 and everyone questions me as to why she's not getting married. We will host a small reception party at our place after a Hindu marriage and we won't tell anyone that you're a Christian. We've found some marriage dates in the next two months.

I was shocked to hear all this. I said, "Dad, it's too soon. You're not giving any time to Jaison. He will have to make all the marriage arrangements by himself. First of all, he'll have to shift back to Delhi. If he doesn't get any job in Delhi, then I'll have to get a job in Chennai. All these things take time and you're giving us no time."

Jaison said, "It's ok Naina, calm down."

My father said, "Ok, if marriage is not possible, then I'd like to do your engagement ceremony in front of my relatives. Both of you can exchange rings after two months and after another month, there'll be a wedding ceremony. This way, you both will get enough time to settle everything. I cannot give you any more time. Jaison, please tell your mother everything."

Jaison said, "Ok Uncle, let me first talk to my mother and then we'll decide. But I want to tell you that my mother has also agreed to our relationship. She wants to discuss it with her relatives. She also needs a 'yes' from everyone."

My father said, "Ok, that sounds great. I hope everything will be fine at your end. Anyway let's eat dinner, you must be hungry!"

Everyone smiled and we sat down to the dinner my mother had made especially for Jaison, after which he left for Chandigarh. I was happy because it seemed that finally I would be united with my love.

Priyanshu and I left for Gurgaon after two days.

After fifteen days Dad called me up. He sounded quite upset. "I told you this boy and his family are not suitable for you. They are very rigid people. Last week I went to see Jaison's mother and his relatives in Chandigarh. All his uncles were trying to be very smart. His mother could not say anything. She seemed very tense, while all his uncles were very rude to me. I asked them to agree to a wedding ceremony at our place according to our customs-because that's how it should be - according to Hindu traditions. But they said no! They wouldn't agree to a Hindu wedding! They want to baptise you and then solemnise a Christian wedding in their church. They feel you won't become a part of Jaison's family unless your wedding is according to their religious customs. They don't understand our feelings at all. After all, you're our only daughter. Your wedding ceremony should be according to our customs and not theirs. I am telling you Naina, it's impossible to even talk to them."

I listened in silence. I could speak only after a few seconds, "Dad, I don't know what actually happened there but no one should be rigid about their culture. Just as I'm your only daughter, he's also the only son of his parents. In this case, both families want that the marriage should be solemnised according to their customs. I suggest we should have both – a Hindu marriage as well as a Christian marriage. I'll talk to Jaison about this."

My father said, "Yes, you should talk to Jaison. When he came over to meet us, he agreed to everything. But now, his relatives are creating this mess. His mother should speak up in this matter. Why is she so scared? She was completely silent when I went to meet her."

After this terrible phone call, I immediately called up Jaison, "What's the matter with our families? Now when my parents have agreed to our marriage, your relatives are creating a mess. They want to have a Christian wedding and my parents want a Hindu wedding. How will we solve this problem? You should talk to your mother to allow both marriages. I have told my father the same thing. Tell Aunty to speak up in front of your relatives. After all, it is her son's marriage. She has the right to express her views."

Jaison said, "Be patient Chunnu. Inter-religious marriages are never so easy, my dear. We both knew that this would happen. My mother is a widow. After my father's death, my uncles were the only ones who supported her during difficult times. She can't be very outspoken in their presence. I'll have to do something. I'll talk to them. You don't worry."

After a few days, Jaison spoke to his relatives but they didn't agree to a Hindu marriage. When Dad called up Jaison's eldest uncle to convince them about the Hindu marriage, he said, "Please don't consider us as part of the Hindu marriage. Only Jaison will come from the boy's side for the Hindu marriage to take seven pheras with Naina. None of us will attend that marriage. This relationship will not be accepted by our church and society. You'll have to go through a Christian marriage only."

My father was having a tough time with Jaison's relatives. As if this was not enough, Jaison also faced a lot of issues in his church. They belonged to a small community. There were two groups – one group was against this marriage and the other was in favour of our marriage. Those opposed to it said that they would not accept a Hindu girl in their community because she would never adjust to their culture.

Jaison's mother then spoke to the priest, "What should I do Acchan? I cannot see my son in pain. He loves that girl so much. I want this marriage to take place. Please help me convince my relatives."

The priest said, "I don't have any problem with this marriage but let this wedding take place in the church .We will first baptise Naina, then we will change her name and teach her about Christianity. Before marriage she and her parents will have to attend church every Sunday. Even after marriage she will have to come to Chandigarh to attend prayers on Sundays. She will have to embrace Christianity. She and her parents will have to sign on a letter that says that Naina has willingly converted to Christianity because she wants to follow this religion."

Jaison's mother told all her relatives about the priest's solution. The relatives were very happy because the priest seemed to be in their favour but it was difficult for Jaison to explain it to me.

He called me up, "Hi Chunnu, how are you?"

"I'm fine, thanks," I said, wondering what was it that he had to tell me.

Jaison continued, "Today, my mother and I had a tough time in church. We talked to the priest about these issues. He has agreed to this marriage. But according to the church regulations, you'll have to be baptised before marriage. Your name will be changed. Before that, you'll have to sign a letter saying that you have converted willingly and according to the wishes of your parents."

Hearing this, I lost my temper and shouted, "What? People know me by this name from my childhood and you're asking me to change my name? You want me to lose my identity forever and above that, you want me to sign on a paper to make it legal. What do you people think of yourselves? Your relatives did not agree to a Hindu marriage. Yet, they want me to make all these sacrifices. Is it fair? Why didn't you say something about it? You could have spoken in my favour. But you did not. How can you forget how much I fought for you? So much so, all my relatives are standing by my side? Look at your relatives and your church. They're so rigid and so tough they don't even want to listen to us."

The conversation turned into a big argument.

Jaison raised his voice, "How can you say that I'm not speaking up for you? You can only talk about your side. But you're not here to see my struggle against our society. At least you have a father who can take a stand for you in front of the others. But look at me – there's no one by my side. I lost my father a few years back. That's why today everyone wants to become my father. Every relative is pressurising us to do whatever they want. It's difficult for a widow to withstand so much pressure. I, being a man, want to handle everything with maturity and patience. Our society is very rigid. If today I don't accept all their conditions, they'll never accept my mother, and the two of us as a part of this society. Let me tell you all these stupid things don't matter to me. I am ok with any kind of marriage. But all these things matter to my mother. After marriage we'll be living separately but my mother will always live in Chandigarh and she has been part of this church since we were kids. She can't go against them. If she does, then these people will boycott her. I don't want to make life difficult for her. Look Naina, all these things are for one time only. I won't ever expect you to follow Christianity in your life. After all, you're going to live life with me and not with these people. And you needn't change your name, it's just a formality."

By now I was highly irritated by all these exchanges between the two families. After a long struggle I was only left with frustration in my mind so I didn't want to understand anything. I disconnected the phone and did not talk to anyone for a couple of days.

After a few days my father called me up.

My father said, "My dear, Jaison's family is not at all cooperative. I've tried my best to tell them that they should neither change your name nor baptise you. But they don't want to understand anything."

I said, "Papa, I've thought of a solution – why don't we go in for a court marriage? It will be simple and the best for all of us. After a court marriage, we can arrange for a lunch party for both families, our friends and all our relatives."

My father said, "I've already found out about the court marriage from a lawyer I know. But I don't want to go in for it because before the court marriage, I'll have to make a public announcement of this marriage through a local newspaper and if till thirty days no one raises any objection to it, then only can both of you get married. My problem is that I don't want to disclose to any one in our society that Jaison is Christian. So I can't give that advertisement in any local Yamuna Nagar newspaper. It's a small town and everyone will ask me questions about your inter-religious marriage. I don't want to answer that. That will bring shame upon me."

I said, "Dad, for God's sake please don't make things any more complicated for us. Why don't you come out of your conservative way of thinking? I live in Gurgaon and here people know that I'm getting married to a Christian guy and nobody asks questions about it. In these metro cities, every second marriage is a love marriage – which is either inter-religious or inter-caste. But people don't really care about it and nobody even has the time to discuss all this. In today's world, you and Jaison's family are still sticking to your orthodox way of thinking. Well, I think I've had enough of it. Now I have only one and the last solution to fix this mess. We'll get married following both traditions - Hindu as well as Christian. Please talk to Jaison's family about it."

My father sounded cross, "Ok, I'll think about it."

After a few days, my father called me up again, "Hello Naina, things are not going as we want. Jaison's family did not agree to what we'd decided last time. I talked to Jaison's uncle again and he said that they will only go in for a Christian wedding. Jaison also called me one day to tell me how his relatives are firm about how they want to go about it. I scolded him and told him that he wasn't bold enough to handle his family. If he cannot stand up to his family then how will he stand by you in future? I told him that I am going to cancel this marriage."

Tears rolled down my eyes and I said, "Papa, I understand your pain and I know why you said this. I'm also feeling frustrated. I cannot fight this anymore. It's already been three months since Jaison came to our home. Now I've lost all hope. I don't even know what to do. I need some time to think over it."

My father comforted me saying, "Don't be tense sweetheart. You did whatever you could. Take your time and tell Jaison the same thing."

I disconnected the phone and called up Jaison.

He picked up the phone and said, "Hi Chunnu. How are you? I called up your Dad last night and he fired me. He sounded really angry. I don't know what to do. Our people have spoilt everything. But I've also told them that if I get married, it will only be to you. No one else."

I replied, "Jaison, I don't want to say anything but let me tell you, my parents also have their dreams about my marriage. They want to observe Hindu customs and rituals. So I also would like to have a Hindu marriage. You try to convince your relatives else we should forget each other. We should end this relationship."

Jaison sounded peeved, "What's this nonsense? You cannot backtrack now. You girls are like this only. When you have to fight, then you start retreating. If you want it to be this way, then I will give you some more time to think about it and after a few days you can tell me your decision."

I disconnected the phone. It was the most difficult time of my life and I wasn't able to handle this situation. I felt heart broken and discouraged. I went through all the motions of everyday life but I felt I was only half alive. All my dreams were shattered.

In frustration I called up Jaison's uncle and gave him a piece of my mind. I said, "Hello Uncle, this is Naina. I hope you know who I am and I don't have to give you my introduction. Uncle, on what basis do you call yourself Jaison's uncle? It seems you don't want us to get married. You aren't standing by his side. You're only showing your rigidity. You're trying to show everyone that you have the upper hand.

Of course you'll feel extremely happy when you convert a girl just because she wants to marry the person she loves. You only care about your feelings and emotions but you don't understand my parents' feelings. You did not give your consent when they said they want to have a Hindu marriage too. God will never forgive you for this."

I disconnected the phone and cried a lot. I decided to take leave for a few days from office and stay with my parents. I packed my luggage, informed my manager and left for Yamuna Nagar. My mother was shocked to see my condition. There were dark circles under my eyes. I had become lean and pale and I looked like a skeleton. All this was because of the stress I was going through. My parents hugged me and asked me not to lose faith in God.

One week passed and there was no phone call from Jaison. I had started missing him very much. Ultimately I couldn't take it anymore and I called him. He sounded furious, "Why have you called me today when you don't want to marry me at all? Please, for God's sake don't cause me any more pain."

I started crying, "Please Jaison, why are you talking to me like this? I still love you a lot."

Jaison said, "It's true that our love can never die. But now it's time to make a decision. You'll have to tell me straight away whether you're ready to marry me or not."

I kept quiet.

Jaison said, "You know what? You're confused. See, I am going to Australia on a business trip for one month. Till such time you can make up your mind."

With that remark Jaison disconnected the phone.

As scheduled, he left for Australia.

My parents also wanted me to forget this relationship. My father told my uncle the same thing. My uncle said, 'You should never allow this marriage to take place. Earlier also I had felt that this was not right but I didn't say anything. I am also worried that if the eldest girl of our family goes in for an inter-religious marriage, then she will set the wrong example for all the other girls of our family. In future, when Naina's cousins grow up, they might also want to marry out of caste or religion and our family values won't remain the same. Let me find a way."

One day I was sitting quietly in my room when my parents came in and held my hand. My father said, "My dear, we can understand your pain and we know it will take you some time before you can tell us your final decision. But we want you to decide as soon as possible so that we may move on with our lives. To help you make up your mind, your uncle has called someone he knows. She also got married to a Christian guy a few years back. She is a Hindu girl. She is coming to see you today. You should talk to her and find out how your life could be after marriage."

I was shocked, "Dad, please. I don't want to talk to anyone. I am myself so depressed and now you expect me to speak to some girl whom I don't even know. How can I handle all this?"

My father said, "There's no harm in talking to her. Please come out and talk to her at least. She's come all the way so we can hardly ask her to go back."

So I was given no choice, I just had to talk to her. My father asked that girl to tell me her story. It seemed that she was waiting for just one indication from me in order to start speaking about her worries.

"I realised that I had taken a wrong decision in life after getting married to a Christian. My man is good but his family is pathetic. They have made my life hell. They forced me to follow their religion. My husband's parents are not good people. They don't even support me financially. I've killed my feelings forever. I suggest that you don't go ahead with this marriage. You might suffer in the same way."

I stared at her and went back to my room. I told my parents, "Dad you know this girl does not have her own standing in life. That's why she is suffering. She can easily find ways to live a happy life but she doesn't want to take any initiative for her happiness. She is totally dependent on her in-laws for everything and cannot say anything to them. That's why her in-laws want her to live her life according to their wishes. Well, I have nothing to do with it. Please don't try to brainwash me. Enough is enough."

After a few days, Jaison called me and said, "Chunnu I love you. I know I was harsh with you. I'm sorry about that. But I have realised that I can't live without you. I love you a lot. You're the only person whom I am missing here. Let me come back and we'll talk again with our families regarding our marriage. You know what! I've also completed my MBA last month. Yes. It's true! Because of all those issues I couldn't tell you."

I was elated, "I love you too Jaison. I agree with you. When are you coming back to India?"

After this call Jaison called me every day. He seemed to be spending most of his money on international calls.

I told my parents that Jaison would be coming to meet them the following month and that we would be finalising our marriage plans.

One month passed before he came back to India and fixed a meeting with my family.

The following Sunday I came to Yamuna Nagar and waited eagerly for Jaison and his mother. It was one o'clock in the afternoon when the doorbell rang. I opened the door expectantly, eager to see Jaison after such a long time. As for Jaison, he blinked his eyes when he saw me. I understood he wanted to tell me that I was looking good in my yellow salwar kameez.

Jaison and his mother settled down and the discussion started. He said to my father, "Uncle, I want to marry Naina."

My father said, 'That's fine Jaison, but we're hurt because many of your relatives said so many things. Moreover, I'm scared that Naina will actually have to change her religion and name forever. Some of your relatives also said that if she wanted to worship her Hindu Gods then she could not do so openly. She would only be allowed to do so within closed doors. We certainly haven't liked this attitude."

My father asked me, "Do you really want to marry Jaison and accept all these conditions?"

I kept quiet for ten minutes, then all my aunts and my mother said, "Speak up now. Don't keep anything in your heart. When we went to their house, their relatives said so many things. Now Jaison and his mother have specially come to us to make the final decision. It is also a final discussion and you have a last chance to clear up everything. After this meeting, both of you will decide if you two still want to get married."

I looked at Jaison and his mother and started speaking, "Aunty, I have a question. Why should I change my name? I've been known by this name since my birth and this is my identity. How would you like it if someone asked you to change Jaison's name and I ask him to change his religion for me?"

Jaison's mother kept quiet. I continued, "After marriage if Jaison comes to my home and wants to read the Bible, then no one can say that he should read the Bible within closed doors because we believe that every person has the freedom to follow his religion. Your relatives said that there will only be a Christian marriage and no Hindu marriage will take place. I am the only daughter of my parents. They have similar feelings. They would like me to get married following our customs. You tell me Aunty, is this fair? Finally I'd like to say that I respect your religion but I will follow my religion throughout my life. I will never change my name. Moreover, I also want a Hindu marriage."

I spoke my mind. There was a long silence after that.

Jaison broke the silence. He said, "I'll get married according to Hindu customs as I care for your parents' feelings. I will not tell my relatives about it. Only my mother, my sister and I will be present for all Hindu marriage rituals."

Jaison's mother said, 'Your baptism before the Christian wedding will only be a formality and your name change will be only for the purpose of the wedding. I will never force you to do anything in your life. You can do whatever you want. My relatives said so many things but I did not say anything to them as I am scared that if I say something then they will do every possible thing to stop this marriage."

Everyone was happy after listening to what Jaison and his mother had to say. Now my father said, "Let's finalise the marriage dates for the Christian as well as the Hindu wedding."

Jaison's mother and my mother hugged each other. My mother gave some money to Jaison as a small present and a sari to Jaison's mother after the marriage dates had been finalised.

The marriage date was finalised in the month of January the following year after my return from USA. I was to leave for USA on an official trip the following month and would return only after three months. Everything went off well at this meeting.

While waiting for my flight at the Indira Gandhi International Airport I spoke to Jaison on the phone. "Dear, this trip will be so joyful for me. I will do lots of shopping - cosmetics and clothes from USA for my marriage. I am waiting for our married life. I'll cook for you, I'll decorate our home. It's such a nice feeling. Please start looking for a job as you'll have to shift to Delhi after marriage."

Jaison said, "Chunnu, our dream is coming true. I am so excited about our new life."

We talked for about an hour. After a few more minutes, I boarded the flight.

I stayed in USA for three months. While I was in the USA, many things were going on at home in India. I was only busy shopping for my marriage on weekends, while my parents were busy making arrangements for my marriage. I kept talking to my family and Jaison. This way I was aware of everything.

After a few days, my brother called me up and told me, "Naina, Dad's given me the responsibility of getting your wedding invitation card printed. He gave me some matter for the card. But I'm feeling very bad about one thing."

Curious, I asked him, "Why, what's happened?"

Priyanshu said, "In the invitation card he wants to get our family name printed but he doesn't want to get Jaison's surname printed. He doesn't even want to get his Dad's name printed because he feels from their name everyone will come to know that you are getting married to a Christian."

I was shocked, "That's such an insult to Jaison. Priyanshu, I don't like this at all. Why does he not want to disclose this inter-religious marriage? Everyone in my office knows about it and also on Jaison's side everyone knows about it, then why can't he disclose this fact to his society. When Jaison comes to know about it, he'll feel very bad. I must talk to Dad about it."

I disconnected and called up my father. I started arguing with him. My father was firm, "I can't disclose to everyone that you are getting married to a Christian. What will everyone say? I don't want to ruin my reputation. You have to understand that, Naina."

I said, "Ok, fine. Then get two types of cards printed. One set of cards will have Jaison's family name and Christian wedding date which can be distributed to our relatives and Jaison's relatives. The other set of cards will have only the Hindu marriage date. You can remove Jaison's surname in those cards and they can be distributed to your friends and colleagues in office. This way your reputation will be saved," I added sarcastically.

I disconnected the phone in anger and turned to God in frustration. "Oh God, why is everything so difficult? Why can't I get married the way I wish to? Why can't I get everyone to see things in the same light?"

Days passed quickly and three months were over but Jaison hadn't been able to find any job in Delhi yet. This was another matter of concern for us.

I came back to India by December end. I distributed the wedding invitation cards to everyone in office and to my friends. They all were very happy and congratulated me, "At last you and Jaison are getting married. This is another achievement for you. Finally the struggle between the two families is coming to an end.

As the news of my marriage spread, I had to face another issue at work. My manager accosted me in a one to one meeting, "Naina, now that you're getting married and your would-be-husband is in Chennai, what are your plans? Could you please tell us clearly so that we may start looking for your replacement? We understand that you will be moving to Chennai."

I smiled, "Sir, I've no plans of going to Chennai. After marriage, we're going to settle in Gurgaon itself. I want to tell you, Sir, that my marriage will affect neither my work nor my efficiency. I'll continue to work in the same manner as I am doing right now."

Three weeks before the wedding date I got a call from my parents. My father said, "Naina, you need to come home. We'll go to Chandigarh together. Your marriage will be solemnised at the same church Jaison and his family go to every Sunday. The priest has asked us to visit the church every Sunday before marriage. You will be baptised this coming Sunday."

The following Sunday I reached Chandigarh with my parents. I saw the small white church with a big cross on top. I entered the church with mixed feelings. Sunday prayers were going on. There were two rows - men on one side and women on the other. Everyone there was Malayalee. All the ladies were wearing sarees and repeating prayers after the priest. The prayers were in Malayalam so I couldn't understand a single word. The priest was standing at the pulpit which had a desk, speakers and it was covered with red curtains. There was a big golden cross in the middle. Two persons were standing on the right side holding incense cups out of which smoke billowed. Prayers went on for the next one hour while I stood there like a statue. I looked at Jaison who was standing on the other side.

After prayers all the people came closer to Jaison and starting talking to him in Malayalam. Some ladies looked at me while talking to him. They teased him while laughing and joking with him. After a few minutes, Jaison came back to me. He said, "Do you know what they were saying?"

I said, "How would I understand? They're speaking in Malayalam, aren't they?"

Jaison said, "They're saying I'm lucky because I've got a beautiful girl."

I smiled, "That's great! But how do they know that I'm your fiancée?"

Jaison said, "The priest had announced our wedding after the prayers. That's how everyone knows about it. These are the same people who had tried to create problems for me. Now look at them – they're congratulating me and telling me I have got a beautiful fiancée. Your beautiful face has stopped their wagging tongues."

"Oh stop teasing me, Jaison. Look, those ladies are coming towards me," I said, a little alarmed.

Some Malayalee ladies came to me and started speaking in Malayalam. I stared at their faces. I wanted to understand what they were saying but I could not understand a single word. Looking at my shocked face, the ladies soon realised that I didn't understand Malayalam. One of them started speaking in English, "Oh! We forgot that you don't understand Malayalam. Anyway, we were just congratulating you on your engagement."

Shyly, I murmured, "Thanks."

One of the ladies said, "Where is your family?" I pointed towards my parents. They were standing on the other side.

Then one lady asked me, "So how many brothers and sisters are you?"

I said, "I have only one brother."

Curious to know more, the lady continued, "What does he do?"

Filling in the blanks for her I said, "He's a mechanical engineer."

Then another lady stepped in, "We've heard from Jaison that you have been to USA two times. That's great. Jaison is so lucky. He's going to marry a beautiful, intelligent and well settled girl who belongs to a good family."

> In our country, I realised, people respect the person who goes abroad. This was happening with me also. Should I be grateful, I wondered. Aloud, I said, "Thanks".

The lady continued, "Welcome to our community. Soon you'll become a new member of this church and very soon you will become a Christian too. You'll have to learn Malayalam, everyone here is Malayalee."

Her words were like a sharp knife piercing my heart. I felt as if someone was trying to control my life. I kept quiet and said nothing. After a few minutes, a priest came into the hall and asked for my parents and me. He started the process of my baptism. He asked us to sign a letter saying that I was getting converted according to my own wish. I didn't want to sign that letter. But I wanted to be united with my love so I had no choice but to go ahead and do it.

After that, he started the rituals for my conversion. He spoke some lines from the Bible in Malayalam and made signs of the cross on my forehead with coconut oil. He poured holy water over my head and announced, "Naina has been baptised."

I turned towards the figure of Christ on the cross and prayed fervently, "God, I respect you a lot. I have full faith in you. I have no issues with any religion. But please give some intelligence to your people. They still don't understand that God is one. Please help this world."

Then I turned back to Jaison. I said, "Jaison, never forget the sacrifice my parents and I have made for our love. I don't have to tell you that I love you very much. You can see that yourself."

After that there was a one hour class to teach me about Christianity. The teacher was well-informed and told me some interesting things about Christianity.

After another hour, the priest and his wife invited us to have lunch. We had fresh dosas, sambar, coconut chatni and tea. It sure was a welcome break.

Then the priest asked me and my parents to come every Sunday to attend church till such time as I got married. I told him that it would be very difficult to come down from Yamuna Nagar to Chandigarh every Sunday as it would be difficult to travel at five o'clock especially in the freezing mornings of January. In fact, we shouldn't be forced to attend the prayers, we should be allowed to do it of our own free will.

But the priest didn't want to listen to us. He started speaking in Malayalam in a loud voice to Jaison's mother. I didn't understand a single word but I could sense that he was showing his anger. Suddenly my mother-in-law went down on her knees and asked for forgiveness.

I lost my temper. I couldn't bear to see a lady humiliate herself this way. I told the priest, "On the one hand you call yourself a messenger of God and on the other, you force your religion on your people. We told you that it was difficult for us to come to church during the winter but you refuse to understand. You yelled at my mother-in-law and she is crying and asking for forgiveness. Don't you feel ashamed that you made a lady cry? And if you want me to attend prayers in church then you should say your prayers in English as I do not understand Malayalam. You are thinking only about yourself and not about us."

After this exchange, the priest became even angrier. Jaison took me to a corner and told me, "Please don't create a scene here. We'll have to follow his instructions. After so many hurdles he has agreed to our marriage, Chunnu. I completely agree with what you say and I know you could not see my mother crying in front of him. But please, for my sake, don't say anything at this moment, just say sorry to him."

I looked at Jaison and tried to understand the whole situation from his point of view. I didn't have any option but to swallow my self respect.

After that big fight, we went back to Yamuna Nagar.

6

Wedding Bells

Only two weeks were left for the wedding. Jaison was busy making all the wedding arrangements and he was very excited about booking his honeymoon package. He had always promised me, "When we get married, I'll take you on a tour of Kerala. Kerala is the land of my ethnic origin and its God's own country. You will simply love that place."

He booked a one week honeymoon package for Kerala and called to give me the news.

I asked Jaison, "Hey, how will we go there - by train?"

Jaison said, "Chunnu my dear, gone are the days when you used to travel in the general compartment of a train. Guess what? I've booked flight tickets for us."

The children had their own group. They were not bothered about anything other than food, games and cartoon shows on television. There were only two bathrooms in the house and the perennial long queues outside the bathrooms were quite amusing.

One corner of the house was occupied by cooks. They made a big brick stove and cooked food in big vessels. They were efficient and cooked for thirty to forty people three times a day. My mother had already decided the menu for the whole week.

Our nights were almost sleepless. All the ladies and the men would get together in one big hall and share silly jokes with each other. Some of the ladies were good at imitating others and they entertained the other guests.

During the day, the ladies would get together and sing and dance for ladies sangeet. My father hired the services of a photographer to capture the special moments of my wedding.

On the day of the Hindu wedding, Jaison, his mother and his sister arrived. I went to the beauty parlour to get ready for the special day and wore a red and golden sari and many ornaments.

Jaison and I met at the wedding venue. He looked at me and smiled. We looked into each other's eyes and I realised that our dream was finally coming true.

We exchanged rings in front of everyone, followed by 'pheras' or the seven steps around the sacred fire. My father performed the ritual of 'kanya daan' and officially gave me away. Only after Jaison had put the 'mangalsootra' around my neck and 'sindoor' in the parting of my hair, were we declared husband and wife. However, we were not allowed to live with each other, as the Christian wedding was still pending. Thus, even after the Hindu wedding, Jaison and I continued to live in our own homes.

A few days later, the Christian wedding took place. Jaison made all the arrangements in Chandigarh for this wedding.

For my Christian wedding, I was dressed in an off white and golden sari that my in-laws had bought from Kerala. I looked like a classic, beautiful Christian bride. When I looked into the mirror, I was excited but at the same time, I was sad. I was happy because I was marrying the love of my life but at the same time, I was sad at the idea of leaving my parents and my home where I had spent my childhood. I was filled with mixed feelings.

The priest performed the wedding rituals. Traditionally, in Malayalee Christian weddings, all the sacred vows are in Malayalam. The minister was a thoughtful person, he knew that my family was North Indian and that we probably would not understand Malayalam, so he asked the priest to speak in English. Our wedding ceremony was completed in one and a half hours. Suddenly it started raining heavily outside. Everyone in the church felt happy and said, "God is showering his blessings on these love birds."

Jaison whispered in my ears, "Chunnu, finally our dream has come true."

After the reception, Jaison, our families and I went to his home in Chandigarh. Members from both families were present there. One of Jaison's aunts came with a coconut with two straws dipped in it. She asked us to sip coconut water from one straw. After that there was another ritual where Jaison and I were asked to drink a glass of milk each. One of his aunts shouted from the back, "Today both of you will have to do hard work, so drink this milk. It will make you strong."

We were embarrassed while everyone laughed. After all the rituals, it was time for my family to leave. At that moment I realised that my life had changed. No longer was I my family's little Naina. From this moment onwards, I would be a married woman and would have my own life and responsibilities. I would be living with the decision that I had taken.

I looked at my mother and my aunts and memories of my childhood flashed in my mind. I did not want to cry but suddenly I burst into tears and hugged my family members tightly. My mother-in-law consoled me. A few minutes later, they had all left. Jaison and I were left alone in the room. It was a tiny room with a single bed inside.

I was getting nervous. Although I knew the person with whom I would be sharing my bed that night, my nervousness was obvious to everyone. My mother-in-law came inside and asked me to change my clothes. As I came out of the room to go into the bathroom, everyone in Jaison's house started staring at me. I got even more nervous and ran back into the room. My sister-in-law came to me and said, "Don't feel nervous 'bhabhi'. You'll be fine." With these words, she left the room.

Jaison locked the room from inside and came towards me. He said, "Naina, come to me." He hugged me tightly and asked me tenderly, "Why are you so scared of me? I'm the same person whom you fell in love with four years back. I care for you and I won't do anything that will make you feel uncomfortable. I'm in no hurry. We have our whole life in front of us. Today is the long awaited moment for us. We should spend this night in each other's arms."

I managed a weak smile after hearing his words. I felt less anxious and relaxed a little. Jaison looked into my eyes and held my hands. He kissed me and placed my head on his lap. He played with my hair and asked me to take a deep breath. I closed my eyes. Soon I slept blissfully. He gently placed my head on the pillow. He hugged me and covered me with the quilt. The next day we left for our honeymoon.

After One Week

Jaison and I held hands while sitting together at the Kochi airport. We were waiting for our respective flights. I kept my head on his shoulder and said, "Jaison, we met four years back and in the past few years, we didn't know if we would ever get married and look, today we are a married couple. Life changes every moment but struggles never end. Look at this moment, I'm feeling so sad because we were together for seven days and we've spent the best moments of our life. But today, you will catch a flight back to Chennai while I'll go back to Gurgaon. I don't know how much I'll have to wait to be with you once again."

Jaison said, "Chunnu, I also feel the same way. I'll try my best to get a good job in Delhi within one month and then we'll live together forever. But till such time, you'll have to continue to stay as a paying guest."

Two hours passed. I had to board my flight that was about to depart. Jaison hugged me and planted a kiss on my lips. His eyes were moist as he said goodbye. I left for Delhi and after half an hour he left for Chennai.

For one month after our marriage, I stayed as a paying guest but I did not like it one bit. Jaison and I spoke every day on the phone. Within that month he got selected in the sales department of one of the IT companies in Delhi while I started looking for a rented apartment. My brother helped me find a nice place in Gurgaon.

We got a beautiful rented house in one of the posh areas in Gurgaon. I was so happy. I had never imagined that I would ever live near the mega mall.

> For a moment my mind went back to the days when Jaison and I would stand near the big glass window of Mega Mall in Gurgaon and look around. I could almost hear Jaison telling me, "Chunnu, in our future together, I dream of living with you in one of these houses. I like this area very much." I remember sighing deeply and telling him, "God alone knows if we will ever get married or live together. I also dream of settling down with you in a nice house in and around this mall."

"You needn't worry about the arrangements. I'll help you arrange your furniture and settle down as Jaison is not here and he'll only be joining us in the next two weeks," Priyanshu's words took me out of my reverie.

After a few days, I moved into my new house. Priyanshu and I arranged everything in the house. The following weekend was the Hindu festival of Holi and Jaison would be coming in from Chennai.

As scheduled, he came back from Chennai one day before Holi. I was so happy to see him. Holi was the first festival after our marriage so according to Hindu customs, this had to be celebrated at my hometown. Thc three of us – Jaison, Priyanshu and I went to Yamuna Nagar and celebrated Holi there. Jaison joined in the celebrations with great gusto and smeared me with so many colours. I looked as if I had adorned myself with war paint. Priyanshu took our pictures. My mother made sweet gujiyas for the family. Jaison ate ten to twelve with great relish. He offered me one and said, "Chunnu, do you remember the day when you brought gujiyas for me when we worked at the Chandigarh office? I ate all of them and then I had to run to the loo so many times."

I burst into laughter. Everyone wanted to know why I was laughing. I had to recount the story once again, much to the delight of my family.

7
Back to My Present

I was laughing loudly while sitting on the stairs, quite lost in my own world. Suddenly, the clouds parted and the sun's warm rays touched my cheeks. It felt good and I was happy to soak it up, as the winter was especially harsh that year. It also brought me out of my reverie and I was jolted back to my present. I realised that I was sitting on the stairs of our house in Gurgaon and not in Yamuna Nagar where my thoughts had taken me.

"Oh dear God, I was so lost in my thoughts that I didn't know where I was," I spoke to myself.

I raised the cup to my lips for a last sip of my coffee but the cup was empty. I had absentmindedly drained it to the last drop. I came inside the bedroom and saw that Jaison was fast asleep. I kissed his forehead lightly but he didn't stir. I sat there, content to just look at him sleeping peacefully like a baby. I couldn't resist kissing him again.

He opened his eyes and said with a bewildered look, "Baby, what are you doing? Aren't you tired after your long journey?" I hugged him, kept my head on his arm and smiled.

"I love you when you smile like that," Jaison said, wide awake now.

"Why?" I wanted to know playfully.

"Because you look so fresh, just like a flower," Jaison said, while playing with my hair.

"Actually, I was elsewhere while you were sleeping. I was walking down memory lane, recollecting, remembering my past," I replied.

"Hmmm......I know everything about you, so I know what you were thinking, Naina. Life comes full circle. It teaches us a lot," Jaison said.

Suddenly his cell phone rang and an international number flashed on the screen.

"Hello, yes?" Jaison's eyebrows were raised questioningly as he picked up his phone.

Pause.

"Hey, how are you? So how are you spending your time alone in Korea?" Jaison asked mischievously.

Pause.

"Yes, yes. Your sister has reached. Do you want to talk to her?" Jaison winked at me.

"Tell him I'll chat with him online in the evening. We can talk for a long time that way," I shouted from the back.

While Jaison was talking to Priyanshu, I took out a few of my childhood photographs with my family - Mom, Dad and Priyanshu. As I looked at them, I thought, "I want to thank you God because you have made life so beautiful. Good days have no value if we don't go through the bad days in our lives. Sometimes, when we have to struggle hard for something, we bemoan our fate and blame you, but at the end, it is this same struggle that brings a smile to our face. It is a smile that heals a thousand wounds, a happiness that refreshes our mind and gives us courage and enthusiasm to start a new life. I have realised that what elders say is true. Life is meaningless without a struggle. To sleep blissfully at night we must work hard during the day.

I have become an inspiration for all my cousins who were born and brought up in Yamuna Nagar and are younger than me. Whenever I talk to them, I tell them about the things that I missed out on in my childhood. I encourage them to come out of their shell and look at things from a new perspective, to be enlightened about things because I believe it is only our thought process that takes us to new highs and lows.

Today, I live the way I want. I chose my freedom. I chose my career and I got married to a person of my choice. I dared to explore life beyond Yamuna Nagar. I met new people and went to so many new places. The best decision I had taken in life was to have stepped out of my cocoon. I had to struggle but that led to my success. In life this is how we grow.

After our marriage, Jaison has become a big favourite in our family. We haven't come across the people who had caused problems in our marriage. I go to the church, temples, gurdwaras and have even visited a masjid. Neither Jaison nor his mother or even my parents have ever stopped me from doing so.

Jaison and Priyanshu have risen in their careers and I wish them all the best for their future. Living in a big city has broadened my vision. It has given me a new perspective. I feel more connected to the world.

As for my parents, they are living their dreams through us. My father's struggle is over because his children are now settled. Today we fulfil all his wishes as it is now time for us to give back to him. My mother enjoys shopping and buys lots of sarees - she doesn't have to hold back any more.

I feel that if you want to do something in your life then you have to do something about it yourself. There are no fairy godmothers waiting in the wings to make all your dreams come true.

I do not know what the future has in store for me but I know the struggle I have faced in my past was not in vain. I am happy I was able to change the thinking of my family to a certain extent. Life sure has a way of teaching you a lot.

Jaison and I have come a long way. We are happy with each other in this new phase of our lives full of new experiences and goals.

Things have changed a lot for all of us. My past has given me a beautiful present and I believe I am going to have a beautiful journey ahead. Remember,

> Darkness is always associated with brightness
>
> Problems are always associated with solutions and
>
> Struggle is always associated with happiness.